RECLAIM YOUR POWER

# RECLAIM YOUR POWER

A GUIDE TO ALLOW YOUR
PASSIONS AND PURPOSE
TO DISCOVER YOU!

## LAUREN
## KRASNODEMBSKI

NEW DEGREE PRESS

RECLAIM YOUR POWER

*A guide to allow your passions and purpose to discover YOU!*

ISBN    978-1-63676-784-0  *Paperback*
        978-1-63676-785-7  *Kindle Ebook*
        978-1-63676-786-4  *Ebook*

*"Step into the fire of self-discovery. This fire will not burn you, it will only burn what you are not."*

MOOJI

# CONTENTS

———

*To my parents, for providing unconditional love.*

*To my mom, for being one of my best teachers.*

*To my dad, for demonstrating what passion for
people, hard work, and grit look like.*

*To the love of my life, for always making my dreams possible.*

*To Brody and Maya, may you always keep your childlike wonder,
feel your passion, and the light and love that lives within you!*

*To my coaches and spiritual guides, your life's work is pure magic.*

*To my cheerleaders, thank you for your unwavering support.*

*To my readers, who inspire me to take messy action, may
you exercise your mind daily until it begins to serve
you, remembering that you are whole and complete
and an instrument of divine light and love.*

# REFLECTIVE QUESTIONS & GROWTH EXERCISES

———

After each chapter, you will find reflective questions that correspond with the themes or lessons presented in that chapter. Please know that you are not alone if you do not have immediate answers, but trust that the answers are within you. Think of the reflective questions and the growth exercises that are found in some chapters as seeds that require water and time if you choose to plant them. Chew on what resonates with you and spit out what doesn't. Consider whether you prefer discussing these with a friend or partner or whether you desire to explore these by yourself. Your inward journey requires *you* to decide what is best for *you*!

# INTRODUCTION

---

*"What are you passionate about?"*

I was asked this question in 2016, and I didn't know the answer. I had everything I wanted—the house, the family, a good-paying job, and an active social life—yet something still felt off. I felt like a caged hamster running tirelessly on the same wheel, going nowhere meaningful. I was empty, drained, and the opposite of passionate.

Deep down, I've always believed we are all placed on this Earth for a reason. I believe that each one of us has a super-power, a purpose, and is full of passion. Yet I found myself frustrated because I didn't know mine, nor did I know how to find the answers. I felt bombarded by the constant hustle of life. There was very little time to seek answers raising two small kids, working more than sixty hours a week, helping care for a parent, sprinkling in social events with friends, and trying to keep the passion of a nineteen-year relationship alive in a somewhat clean home. Unable to continue living from a depleted tank, I was determined to find answers by going on an inward quest.

Not knowing what I liked to do and having a job that I didn't love seemed abnormal to me, but I discovered a 2017 Gallup poll that found 85 percent of people say they are unhappy with their jobs. Apparently, I wasn't alone. I found myself in jobs that drained my energy.

Our current society defines us by what we accomplish, how much money we make, and how many material possessions we own. We have been consciously and unconsciously conditioned that we are not enough. Mindfulness, balance, happiness, and inner peace are not things we are taught; rather, we are conditioned to think they're things that can be bought if you work hard enough. It is rare to find self-care on the to-do list, given all of life's competing priorities. Day by day, we give our energy and power away. We merely survive rather than thrive.

I believe there are hidden gems, gifts, and passions within all of us that go undiscovered or not fully expressed because we are so busy *doing* rather than *living* our truest desires. I, like so many people, was not even aware of my own passions and desires. My achievements gave me "outward" success and financial stability. I found myself paralyzed to take risks or see the possibilities around me.

I've learned that our thoughts and belief systems, shaped by our makeup and life experience, can hold us captive and diminish the confidence within us. Feelings of self-doubt creep in, and the belief of "I am not enough" is definitive. It is not uncommon to question your true abilities. Imposter syndrome affects over 70 percent of the population, which I've found sucks the joy and fulfillment out of life (Craig, 2018). As I write this book in the midst of 2020, anxiety and depression are at an all-time high. Fear and limiting beliefs coupled with a lack of boundaries and the need to please others keep us stuck and make us slaves to societal norms.

I wrote this book because I know I'm not alone. I know I'm not the only busy, driven woman who yearns for inner peace, passion, and purpose. I know I'm not the only one who has repeated negative patterns that aren't serving me or my life.

By pressing pause and becoming an observer of my own life, I opened the door for a deep inward journey. Between hiring a soul exploration life coach, making conscious discoveries of my inner thoughts like: *Holy shit, all of my thoughts are anxiety provoked and negative,* and learning how to meditate and practice yoga, I finally began to move past my fears and limiting beliefs. I found my authentic self. As a result, my passions and purpose naturally found me.

I believe we don't find our passions and purpose; they discover us through the self-discovery process. My desire is that this book will give you the inspiration to make yourself a priority, to help you move past your limiting mind so that you can trust your instincts and take action from your heart space.

I hope this book can serve as a guide, providing you the tools to begin or deepen your self-discovery process, which will allow you to become conscious of what is blocking you from taking action and designing a life you love. I trust the stories, quotes, reflective questions, and growth exercises sprinkled throughout this book will help you reclaim your own power so that you can show up with a renewed zest for your life, which will naturally allow your passions and purpose to find *you.*

Now is the time to get off the hamster wheel and go within. The world needs *your* hidden gems, passions, and purpose to shine!

Light and love,
Lauren

# CHAPTER 1

# OH SHIT

---

*"Knowing yourself is the beginning of all wisdom."*

ARISTOTLE

It was a cold, snowy evening in December. I was in the back seat of my mom's car as she drove my sister and me to a palm reader's house. She gifted us readings as an early Christmas present. We had enough material things, and she thought it would be a fun, memorable experience. We were excited to hear what this mystical lady who referred to herself as "The Passionate Palmist" would say. I was especially curious and intrigued. I had been feeling cloudy, and I constantly questioned whether I was on the right path. I felt deep inside that I was supposed to be doing something else, but I had no idea what.

From the outside, my life looked great. I created the life that many people dream of: married to my high school sweetheart and blessed with a healthy son and daughter, a cozy home, loving family and friends, and the opportunity to travel. I even worked my way up the corporate ladder as a successful health care privacy attorney.

*And yet, a little voice would whisper: Something isn't right,*
*Lauren. Life shouldn't feel this stressful and draining. Why*
*are you feeling so tired and unfulfilled? Isn't this what you*
*wanted? Just be grateful. So many people have it harder than*
*you. Suck it up. Keep going.*

Deep down, I knew life had more to offer. I just couldn't pinpoint what I needed to stop all of the negative feelings. I was feverishly running on a hamster wheel with no true direction or purpose in sight. My mom parked the car in front of a normal-looking apartment.

*Finally, we are here.*

Surely, the Passionate Palmist would be able to tell me what I needed to do or how I could fix the way I was feeling. After all, I had become an expert fixer, people pleaser, and avid achiever.

*Were fixing and people pleasing the reasons why I felt so*
*hardened and exhausted, completely overworked, and under-*
*whelmed with life?*

We rang the doorbell. I patiently waited for the Passionate Palmist to open her front door as snowflakes fell onto my coat. I had absolutely no idea that walking through her door would completely change the trajectory of my life. What was supposed to be a fun and lighthearted Christmas gift turned into an outing that I would continue to think about every day over the next three years.

The door opened. "Wow, the snow is really coming down out there! Come on in," the Passionate Palmist said as she opened her door. She then quickly ushered us into her warm apartment. As we took off our jackets, I couldn't help but notice the smell of burning incense as she led us down a narrow hallway toward a back room.

On one side of the tiny room sat a medium-sized rectangular desk that had three chairs lined up on the other side. The palmist motioned for us to sit. My sister, Kate, sat in the middle chair and placed her hands on the table.

The palmist began studying the lines on Kate's hands with an intense look and said, "You are very compassionate and like to give and help others."

My sister nodded her head. "Yes, I am a teacher at a low-income school. Although, I am not sure it is the right fit anymore. I feel discouraged that I cannot help the children more, and I am frustrated by how much work there is to do."

The Passionate Palmist pressed her lips together and ran her index finger over her hands. "But if you are not giving back to the world, you will feel unfulfilled. I encourage you to stick this out and create boundaries for yourself. Focus on the lives you are touching versus what you can't fix."

"Okay," said my sister. "Boundaries are something I am working on since it's hard for me to compartmentalize my work and home life. Do you see anything in my lines about marriage? My boyfriend is taking his time to propose."

"He feels like a good fit. He does his own thing on his own time. Stay patient with him and things will come together. The more you rush him, the more he will pull away."

This seemed to resonate with Kate, as she grinned and nodded in agreement. I became fascinated by the palmist's ability to make money reading hands. Everything she was sharing with my sister seemed spot on. I eagerly awaited my turn, extremely hopeful that I would receive some answers and guidance on how to feel more fulfilled.

It was my turn for the hot seat. I held out both of my hands, and the palmist gently grabbed my right hand and flipped it over so my palm was facing up. As she studied its engrained lines, she stroked each line with her index finger.

She asked, "Do you see this long line that splits off into a V shape? You have a writer's fork. You have a natural ability to write."

My hope for answers instantly shattered.

*I am so happy I didn't spend my money on this because this chick has no idea what the hell she is talking about!*

I didn't want to hurt her feelings, so I just smiled and said, "That is an interesting observation."

*A writer? What is she talking about?*

I thought about all of the work emails and memos that took me hours to compose. I wrote something only to delete it fifty times. After sending, paranoia would set in about how many words I had misspelled or whether I had screwed up an apostrophe. I was not a writer. I didn't enjoy writing. And I absolutely wasn't any good at it.

I couldn't even write simple greeting cards. I remembered the time I bought an anniversary card for my husband. I knew in my heart what I wanted to say, but the words just wouldn't come. So I wrote something generic and called it a day.

The Passionate Palmist continued to study the lines on my hands, pausing to write down a few notes on the piece of paper next to her. Just as I was dismissing the value of this reading, she hit me with a question that quickly grabbed my attention.

The room fell silent as she looked me dead in the eye and asked, "So tell me, what is it that you are passionate about?"

I looked at her dumbfounded. I must have looked like a deer in headlights.

"Passionate? I am not even sure I know what that word means." I started to feel a knot forming in the back of my throat. I looked to my mom and sister, hoping they could answer for me. They looked back at me with blank stares. The silence felt like an eternity.

"I guess I am passionate about my family, but is that even considered a passion?"

*What the hell is a passion anyway? Are there right and wrong answers? Why do I doubt myself so much?*

The palmist watched my body language as I continued to look at my mom and sister for the answers. "Well, what is it that you like to do?" the palmist asked.

*Jesus, lady! Aren't we paying you to tell me these things? Why am I being interrogated here?*

My body felt warm, and I let out a deep sigh.

*How is it that I don't know what it is I like to do at thirty-two years old?*

Without thinking, I muttered, "I do enjoy drinking with my friends, which is likely not a good answer."

*Drinking—seriously, that is your answer?*

My sister sat up and said, "Well, you are really good at getting shit done, and you like cooking for people."

She was right. I was the ultimate doer. I loved food and people and got a sick sense of satisfaction while putting pen to paper as I crossed out a line item. But then it hit me. I had an "oh shit" moment.

*Is my life seriously just one long-ass list of "to-dos"?*

My head started to spin.

*What do I like to do? Surely crossing things off a list isn't something I could enjoy.*

The palmist began taking notes on a piece of paper that had four headings in bold, black letters that read:

- **Life Purpose**
- **Life Lesson**
- **Heart Type**
- **Gifts/Talents/Other Notes**

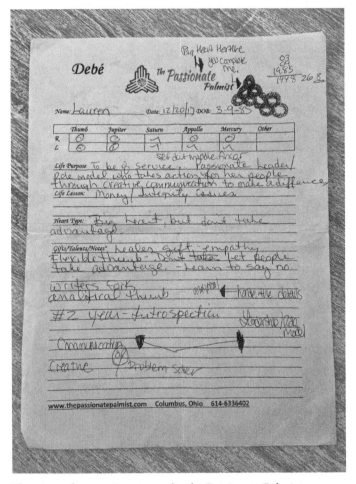

The piece of paper given to me by the Passionate Palmist

"Your life's purpose is to be of service. You are a passionate leader and role model who takes action for her people through creative communication to make a difference."

*This is a joke!*

I heard creative communication and my eyes began to roll. I was positive there was not a creative bone in my body. I was analytical, rigid at times, and task oriented. How could creative communications seriously be my life's purpose?

"Your life lessons are around money and integrity."

*Well, she got the money part right. Integrity issues? What does that even mean? I spent my life doing the right thing, constantly attending to others, and always keeping my word.*

The palmist smiled as she looked at me. "You have a big heart, but you need to stop letting people take advantage of you by learning how to say no."

*Ouch. Do I really let people take advantage of me? What would people think of me if I said no?*

Touching my middle finger, she said, "There is a lot of self-doubt here." Her fingers slowly drifted to my thumbs. "Your thumbs show that you are analytical and able to handle the details. They show you are flexible with your approach. You also have a healer gift of empathy, and I am seeing a two-year period of introspection."

As she stood up from her chair, she handed me the piece of paper and concluded the reading by telling me, "When you discover your passions, things will fall into place."

We walked down her narrow, dark hallway in silence as we headed for our coats. That cloudy and confused feeling that I had walking into her house had elevated tenfold. I couldn't make heads nor tails of what she had told me. I didn't feel a single bit closer to knowing if I was on the right path. In fact, I felt worse. I left with a pit in my stomach, realizing I had absolutely no idea who I was or what I liked to do.

As my mom drove us home, I carefully studied the piece of paper, trying to make sense of it. That evening, I folded it up and stuffed it in one of the six untouched journals that sat tucked away in my nightstand. *When was there time to journal?* Even if I found the time, I wouldn't know what to write.

As I shut my nightstand, I decided to go on an inward quest for answers. I couldn't stop thinking about the palmist's question, "What is it that you are passionate about?" I had no idea how to figure it out, but my heart wanted answers. After placing the piece of paper into one of my journals, I completely forgot about everything she had written down. I was too consumed trying to find answers for what it was that I was passionate about. It wasn't until years later, when it fell out of my journal and onto the floor, that it all made sense.

**REFLECTIVE QUESTIONS**
- What are you passionate about?
- List the top five things that excite you because you like to do them.
- If money didn't matter, how would you spend your time?

# CHAPTER 2

# YOUR LIFE IS NOW

---

*"The trouble is, you think you have time."*

BUDDHA

The gentle man with the biggest sparkling white smile was gone, just like that. My husband and I were driving home from our first three-night getaway since having our second child, listening to *The Subtle Art of Not Giving a F*ck*. My phone rang. It was one of my best friends from my childhood. I smiled as I picked up the call.

My smile quickly disappeared as she said, "I have bad news. Tony just died. He was shot responding to a domestic violence call."

My mouth opened as I gazed out the window. I could barely catch my breath.

*Did she just tell me that our day care provider's husband died? The one who was planning to walk his daughter down the aisle in a few months and retire next year?*

I needed more answers.

*How did this happen? Why?*

All I could think about was Tony's family and hugging my kids. I stared out the window, motionless, unable to speak.

As my husband continued to drive, I thought about how I was going to tell my son that he wouldn't be eating lunch with Tony anymore. I was heartbroken to think that I wouldn't see him again. As soon as we got home, I turned on the TV to find the shooting blasted across every news channel. I tried changing the channel, but there was no escaping it. I sat on my couch as pictures of the scene and Tony's face stared back at me. Tears began falling from my face. The flood of tears didn't stop for weeks. It dawned on me that I hadn't cried in over a year and a half.

The community organized prayer gatherings. I sat on the high school gymnasium bleachers with tissues in hand, barely able to move because we were packed in like a can of sardines. Person after person shared about Tony's compassion and his love for people. Each story left another knot in my stomach. As I drove home, my tears turned to sobs. I tried to catch my breath as I wiped the snot pouring from my nose onto my sleeve.

*What's wrong with me? Why can't I pull myself together?*

I had people in my own family pass away, and I couldn't recall grieving like this.

*What are you grieving, Lauren?*

The answer was clear. If I died tomorrow, I believed I would be remembered as a stressed-out woman who worked all of the time and who was too busy for the things that really mattered. A woman who tried to please everyone else around her while focusing on everything she didn't get to—a woman who lived a good—but not great—life because she didn't fully explore the voices within telling her something wasn't right.

It was as if I was trying to swallow a handful of pills at the same time without any water. I felt like I was choking. At that very moment, the Passionate Palmist's voice came to me. *What is it that you are passionate about?*

It had been a year since she had asked me that question. While I continued to think about the question daily and even vocalized to others that I was searching for my passion, I realized that fourteen months had gone by and I had not taken a single action step. I had only thought about the question in my head. There I was, wasting precious heartbeats, letting life get the best of me as I fed my fears of not being enough. Tony's death was a wake-up call that my life was *now*.

A GoFundMe page was set up to support Tony's family. My heart felt called to help beyond just a financial donation. I tried to think of other ways I could support and decided to meet with my company's community engagement team to see if they would match donations or if they had ideas for continued support. I liked the idea. It felt right, but my plate was full, my anxiety was through the roof with all of the unanswered emails in my inbox, and I was emotionally drained.

As I started to answer a few of those emails, I began to talk myself out of the idea because I didn't have time.

*There you go again, Lauren. You can't even spend time on something that actually matters, something that you actually want to do? How do you think you are going to find your passion answering emails?*

Fighting the urge to respond to more emails, I stopped what I was doing and carefully crafted an email to the community engagement team. It was a small yet big step that felt closer to my truth.

## REFLECTIVE QUESTIONS

- If you died tomorrow, how would you like to be remembered?
- Name three things that are preventing you from living your heart's desires *now*. What is one step you can take today to align with your desires?
- When was the last time you cried or allowed yourself to feel and accept your emotions?

# CHAPTER 3

# THE MERRY-GO-
# ROUND OF CYCLES

---

*"Where energy goes, energy grows."*

LISA NICHOLS

I knew something needed to change. I was physically exhausted and emotionally empty. With Tony's death at the forefront of my mind, I was reevaluating how I was living my life. Constantly putting out fires and attending to everyone else's needs but my own clearly wasn't working. Life was running me; I wasn't running it.

One day, my work friend April knocked on my office door as I was pouring freshly pumped breast milk into a Styrofoam cup since I had forgotten the bottle at home.

"Ah, so good to see you. Things have been so crazy!"

April always had a calming presence and shared the best advice.

With a half-smile, I asked, "So are you ready for this morning's bitch session?"

April patiently listened as I explained how I couldn't keep up with life.

"Lauren, you need to give yourself a break," she said. "You are attending to two little people, one who isn't even sleeping through the night. You are breastfeeding and trying to keep up with more business than you can count on two hands. Not to mention you're helping to care for your dad, preventing his office building from going under, and managing to squeeze in a few workouts."

Despite hearing my intense laundry list repeated back to me, I just couldn't seem to give myself a break. "Something has to give, especially at work. I'm totally overwhelmed and feel utterly incompetent," I said.

"What are you talking about? You have taught me so many things! I think you have imposter syndrome."

"What the hell is that?" I asked.

"Imposter syndrome is when you feel like you're a fraud. You may feel as if someone is going to catch you for not knowing what you are doing. Perhaps you believe your success is due to mere luck rather than your own skills and qualifications. It is common in high-achieving professionals and women."

I quickly googled imposter syndrome. "You are totally right. This *is* me!"

"So what are you going to do about feeling so overwhelmed?" April asked.

"I'm going to schedule a meeting with my boss because something has to be taken off my plate."

April looked at me with a smile. "I think that is a really good idea. What do you plan to say?"

"I have no clue."

I had to come up with plan B, which required facts and objectives. I couldn't wing this one hoping that I could articulate my feelings, and I sure as hell wasn't about to use the new-mom card or this imposter syndrome revelation.

In preparation for the meeting, I instinctively grabbed a journal and drew a line down the center of the page. For the next month, I began tracking my thoughts, feelings, and energy throughout the day. The left-hand column read "Drains My Energy" and the right-hand column "Brings Me Energy." I found myself writing short little notes based on the task at hand and my feelings or thoughts associated with it.

| DRAINS MY ENERGY | BRINGS ME ENERGY |
|---|---|
| Received email from outside counsel - Anxious and frustrated that I couldn't quickly comprehend the email | Working out - Clears my mind and brings me strength |
| | Being outside - I feel more alive |
| Finished a work memo - Unfulfilled because I don't believe my work adds value or meaning to the world | Cuddling with the kids - I feel at peace |
| | Weekend - I have more control over my time |
| Morning phone calls on my way into work re: dad's medical building - Depletes my energy before my workday begins | Sleep - My mind feels clear and calm when I first wake up in the morning |
| Inside the office all day - No time to be outside or do what I want | Checking something off my to-do list - Brings a sense of satisfaction and relief |
| Responsible for too many businesses - Makes me feel like I am doing half ass work trying to accommodate everyone | |
| Rushing the kids out of the house to get to work - I feel sad and guilty | |
| Packing the kids lunches - Annoyed because it takes too much time | |
| Too many things on my to-do list - Frustrated because I always feel behind | |

I began to see cyclical patterns that repeated themselves. Each note by itself was subtle. Had I not written everything down, it is unlikely I would have been able to see the clear patterns. My thoughts, feelings, and actions would have blended into the next day, and my autopilot programming would have continued. This exercise allowed me to become an observer of my own life, which allowed me to reclaim some of my power by breaking the cycle of what drained my energy. It increased my consciousness and allowed me to move away from being a victim of the thoughts and emotions that held me captive. Using my notes, I drew a circle with little tallies. Each tally represented my repetitive cycle. The first tally would always start with a task, often one that required uninterrupted time, research, and analysis. I'd then be given or would set an unrealistic goal. The task would make it onto the mile-long to-do list, forcing me to work on tasks that preceded it. Analysis and/or paralysis would ensue because I didn't know where to begin. I'd procrastinate because it didn't interest me and I dreaded doing it. I would be distracted and discouraged by the other emails pouring in. Time would pass, causing my anxiety to rise since nothing was getting accomplished. Out of fear of failing or letting someone down, I would push myself to deliver, often over-preparing and seeking validation through the process.

New Task

Exhausted / Unfulfilled

Time needed to complete task

Over-preparing to deliver excellence

Unrealistic goal

Pushing myself to deliver

New task added to list

Fear of failing or letting someone down

Forced to work on previously submitted tasks

Anxiety Increases

Analysis/ Paralysis/ Procrastination

Discouraged/ Frustrated/ Distracted

Over-preparing took place after-hours. I began to realize I was not able to over-prepare like I once had since my extra time was now dedicated to my kids and sleepless nights. Anxiety and stress would cause me to stuff my feelings and overeat. Overeating caused more fatigue. Self-doubt crept in, and I found the need to check my work with others because I was afraid of making a mistake or having to defend my work. This vicious cycle often yielded a positive outcome, which reinforced continuing the cycle. If I received praise, I discounted it, attributing the compliment to my "extra" work or the input I received from others. I felt resentful and over-whelmed by my to-do list. I felt sad that I wasn't outside with my kids. The entire cycle was a self-fulfilling prophecy that sucked the life out of my soul.

Two days before the big meeting with my boss, I found myself on my habitual morning phone call with my mom. "Hey honey, how are you doing?"

"Eh, okay. Trying to prepare for a big meeting with my boss to see what can be taken off my plate."

"Good for you, but I still think you need to consider going part-time."

My blood began to boil! I was pissed by her comment. Her suggestion didn't make it in one ear before I pushed my foot on the gas pedal.

*It must be nice not to have to go to work each day and be able to go on vacation whenever you want. Did she forget that part-time isn't exactly a thing for my position and that I have kids and school loans to pay for?*

Part-time never crossed my mind. Partially because deep down, I knew I would struggle to complete a full-time workload in half the time for half the pay. Not to mention, I was certain my company wouldn't entertain the idea for my position, so why even bother asking?

I didn't realize this until much later in my life, but I had a deep fear of losing or quitting my job. I didn't think part-time jobs existed for the work I did, and I was fearful that working part-time wouldn't bring me the security I craved.

*How would I provide for my kids if I quit my job?*

Looking back, my defensiveness and resentment toward my mom were clues that the flexibility and freedom she had were things I desired. I wasn't able to see this at the time. All I knew how to do was to push harder when things got tough.

As I sat across from my boss, I made a clear request that something needed to be taken off my plate. Without providing details about my true feelings about my work, I walked her through my vicious cycle. She listened intently with empathy. We brainstormed various tasks that I could outsource to outside counsel, and she recommended I work from home one day a week. While outsourcing removed a few things from my to-do list, it didn't take away my feelings that I was a fraud. It also didn't solve the unfulfillment I associated with my work.

As I continued to read more about imposter syndrome, I was shocked to see that 70 percent of people suffer from this phenomenon (Craig, 2018).

Valerie Young, EdD, author, speaker, and leading expert on impostor syndrome, found that when it comes to feeling competent, people who feel like impostors hold themselves to impossibly high standards.

She identified five Competence Types:

1. **Perfectionist**: Someone with high expectations, and when small mistakes are made, they feel like a failure.

2. **Superwoman/Superman**: In addition to crushing it at work, they think they should excel in multiple roles—parent, partner, homemaker, friend, and community volunteer.

3. **The Natural Genius**: Because they view competence as being about "ease and speed," if they struggle to master something, they judge themselves as lacking.

4. **The Soloist**: Because they think accomplishments only count if they do everything themselves; asking for help proves they're a fraud.

5. **Expert**: Because they believe they need to know 150 percent, they may not apply for jobs or start a business. They may constantly seek out additional certifications, training, or research to feel qualified.

Young indicates, "The only way to stop feeling like an impostor is to stop thinking like an impostor." Young found non-imposters think differently about three specific things: competence, failure, and fear. For example, non-imposters know that nothing is going to be perfect the first time, and they are confident in what they know. They view feedback as a gift, and they do not try to prove that they've got this; they just go for it!

In Young's book, *The Secret Thoughts of Successful Women: Why Capable People Suffer from the Impostor Syndrome and How to Thrive in Spite of It*, she interviewed a woman who was debating whether or not to take a promotion. The woman's self-doubt of whether she could do the job started to creep in, and Young said to her, "Well, maybe you just don't really want it." This caught the woman off guard.

Young has found that for imposters, ambivalence can be easily confused with a lack of confidence. One can get so consumed by the thoughts of self-doubt that other voices get drowned out. Those other voices tend to lend themselves to who we are and what we actually want rather than whether we can do it. Young says the question becomes, "Am I afraid because I don't think I can do it—or is it because I don't want 'it'?"

As a recovering imposter myself, I realized that I allowed my imposter feelings to take over and run my life because I had an intense need for financial security, control, and achievement. I regained my power each time I shifted my cycle from believing that I wasn't enough to training my mind to focus on what I did accomplish. I began to spend less energy feeding my fears of failing and more energy on failing fast and focusing on what I desired. Slowly but surely,

I began to take action toward searching for a new job that aligned with my desires.

**REFLECTIVE QUESTIONS**

- Do you suffer from imposter syndrome? If so, list three life experiences that may have contributed to this phenomenon.
- Are you using your time and thoughts to grow things that bring you energy or drain you?
- Who do you resent and why? Use this list as a potential clue and as a stepping-stone to your true desires.

**GROWTH EXERCISE**

- Document your thoughts, energy, and patterns to understand your habitual cycles. Do this over a period of several days so that you can notice trends.

| DRAINS MY ENERGY | BRINGS ME ENERGY |
| --- | --- |
| | |

# CHAPTER 4

# YOU'RE WORTH IT

———

*"The best investment you can make is in yourself."*

WARREN BUFFET

Laying in my bed, mindlessly scrolling on Instagram, I couldn't stop staring at an old friend's picture who was cooking at some mystical life clarity retreat in the mountains. She looked so happy and peaceful! It had been a day—a month for that matter—and I finally made the decision that enough was enough. I needed to invest more time in myself by looking for jobs that would pay market price for my expertise, pay for training and certifications, and afford me flexible working hours.

I realized I wasn't using my full potential when searching for other jobs because I wasn't sure if I was worth more money. Plus, looking for a new gig was a part-time job, and I was already juggling all of the things. Shortly after the meeting with my boss, she shared that she would be leaving the company and moving across the country. We made a great team and she felt like my lifeline. Her decision to leave kicked my search into high gear.

It was fall, which meant taking inventory of the kids' closets to ensure they had warm clothes that fit and my annual roommate girls' trip. I had zero energy for either. Instead of packing, I continued to lay on my bed, drained, thinking about the two hours of work I still had to complete. It was already 9:00 p.m. and I just wanted to go to sleep. Unable to think about anything else but this mystical retreat, I found myself stalking my friend's post.

My husband often told me I'd make a great detective, so I decided to put those skills to the test. It wasn't long before I was reading this mystical lady's website. Her name was Mariko Frederick. She was the owner of Soul Priority. She claimed to be a spiritual soul-purpose coach who had died and come back to life. As I scrolled through her Instagram account, I found myself hanging on words like #getunstuck, #spiritualhealer, #lifeclarityretreat, #soulgrowth, and #higherconsciousness. Mariko's pictures were soothing, earthy, and full of nature and tranquility.

I needed Mariko in my life, and I needed her now! I sent that friend Adrienne a private message, even though we hadn't spoken in over five years since she had moved to California after her boyfriend had taken his own life. Her boyfriend was my husband's best friend, which is how we knew each other. Trying to play it cool, I hit send, hoping she would give me the lowdown on Mariko and this retreat.

Within a minute, Adrienne said, "OMG, Lauren, it is so good to hear from you. I always love seeing pictures of you and your adorable family." We quickly caught up and she highly recommended Mariko.

"I feel like Mariko has special powers," she said. "I worked with her for a bit, and she helped me work through a number of difficult things that I was holding on to. I can totally introduce the two of you if you are interested."

Mariko was exactly who I needed in my life to help me understand why I felt so off. I couldn't help but notice that I was hoping that someone else would give me the answers just like the Passionate Palmist.

I mustered up the endurance to finish my last two hours of work and gathered my outfits for the trip with hope in sight. I had mixed feelings about going, as there was so much going on. I wasn't sure if I'd be able to relax and enjoy it. But flights were booked, lodging was secured, and there was a twinkle of hope that it would be the rejuvenation I needed. Knowing my husband was amazing with the kids put my mind at ease. So off I went, wheels up, headed for Provincetown, the northern tip of Cape Cod.

All six college roommates met up at a swanky restaurant in Boston for a fabulous mimosa lunch before catching the ferry over to Ptown. I was thankful for those mimosas. They took the edge off and helped me feel more like myself—at least so I thought. Although I was on paid time off, I couldn't help but watch my work phone pile up with emails. Each time I went to the bathroom, I'd attempt to answer as many as I could in an effort to reduce my anxiety.

It wasn't long before we arrived at our quaint three-story house that was situated right downtown. Our patio backed up to the beach and the calm water. I found myself sharing a room with my best friend, Blair. When I threw my bag over to the corner of our room, failing to unpack it, Blair gave me an odd look. I was notorious for immediately unpacking my stuff so that I would feel settled. It was a clear sign that I was not myself.

As we were getting ready for dinner, I received a text from Mariko. It read, "If you are free, I can call you at 1:00 p.m. PST for a quick introduction call to see if we're a good fit for each other." I was so desperate to work with her that I didn't care about taking a call on vacation.

My fingers quickly texted back, "That will work."

As I was texting Mariko, Blair looked at me and said, "Hello! Are you even here? You've barely said a word. What do you want to do tonight?" Confused by her comment, I gave her a grin and took a sip of my wine.

"I don't care. I thought the girls said we were going to dinner."

"True. Well, if you wanna go out after dinner, we should," she said as she finished getting herself ready.

We found ourselves enjoying dinner and doing a round-robin of our lives. It felt so good to be connected with everyone again. I couldn't help but take in the fresh air and the picturesque town filled with beautiful houses, flowers, and peaceful water that surrounded us. However, as the spotlight pivoted to me, I didn't know what to say. I found myself unable to articulate how I was feeling and merely provided the laundry list of things I was handling.

I started to tear up. "I am not in a good place right now. I've been crying almost every day on my way to work. I'm exhausted all of the time, and life just feels heavy. Brian and the kids are doing great."

I paused to take a sip of my wine.

"I just can't figure out exactly what I need. I've started applying for new jobs, which has added to my invisible load. I've also hired a property manager who is amazing. She is helping me handle my dad's business stuff. But I'm still cleaning the bathrooms in my dad's office building each morning before I go to work. We are trying to save money since we are concerned the building will go under. The lawyers say my dad could be financially responsible based on the paperwork he signed when he was experiencing a manic phase. It's possible the bank could go after my dad's disability money, which would leave my mom and dad high and dry. I honestly can't even go there. I know they say 'fake it until you make it,' but there is just no more faking it anymore. I feel like there is something else I want to do with my life, but I have no idea what. I found this mystical life coach online, and I'm talking with her tomorrow."

My roommates were all staring right at me—each one carefully assessing how to best respond. Finally, Jen, who was sitting directly across from me, chimed in with her sweet voice, "I'm really sorry you are feeling this way. Just hearing you talk about it drains me. I'm glad you are starting to delegate things and have found someone that can help you."

Saturday afternoon rolled around, and we ventured off on bikes to check out a nearby beach. As we drifted off the beaten path, I was nervous that I wouldn't have cell service and would miss my introduction call with Mariko. Our call was quickly approaching, so I walked up to the top of a hill to increase my cell signal. As I was walking, my phone rang.

"Hi Lauren, it's Mariko! How are you?"

Her voice was upbeat and calming. "Doing pretty good. I am on vacation with my college roommates."

"Oh, how fun! I won't keep you too long, but I like to jump on a call with potential clients before they hire me so that I can determine whether or not I can help. So, tell me . . . how can I help you?"

"Well, I am not entirely sure, but Adrienne tells me wonderful things about you. Lately, I've been feeling very run down and not myself. I have this feeling inside that I'm supposed to be doing something else, but I don't know what it is or how to find it. I was told that once I figured out what I am passionate about, everything would naturally come together."

"I see." The other end of the line fell silent.

"Are you still there?" I asked.

"Yes. I should have explained that I read your energy over the phone and perform clearing work on your causal and astral body."

*Causal and astral body? Are we speaking a different language?*

"I do think I can help you, and I can get you in three weeks from now. I charge $1,500 for a four-hour intensive session. Will that work for you?"

"Yes!" I blurted out.

"Make sure you are in a comfortable space for our call. Somewhere that you feel relaxed and where you won't be interrupted. Oh, and don't forget to fuel your body with healthy food and water the week leading up to our call. It helps me cleanse your energy."

I didn't understand her food comment, but I thanked her and walked back down the hill to meet my friends. I couldn't believe I had just verbally agreed to pay that much money for only four hours of her time, but she had provided me with hope.

I blinked and the weekend was over. While I got some rejuvenation, it wasn't quite the rejuvenation I needed, given I drank like a fish and stayed up way too late each night.

As we packed up our bags, Blair looked at me and said, "I am not sure if you are there, but it is time to leave. Grab your bags."

It hadn't dawned on me why she was talking to me like that. I thought I did a good job showing up as Lauren, the bubbly, party-hearty, outgoing girl with a smile on her face.

College roommate trip in Provincetown

Looking back, I find it sad how out of touch I was with my own reality. Sure, I knew things were off, but I didn't fully comprehend the extent because I had learned to disassociate from my feelings. I had perfected making things look easy, like everything was just fine. I had become a fixer, a doer that people depended on, and I didn't take that responsibility lightly. I hated letting anyone down, especially because I enjoyed helping other people. Life had snuck up on me. Slowly but surely, I kept adding more weight over time and I became immune to how much I was carrying. It's not ironic that outsiders around me could see this more clearly.

On the ferry ride home from Ptown to Boston, my roommate Erin asked, "So how much are you paying this lady you want to work with?"

"You don't want to know." When I stated the price, Erin's eyes got big, and her mouth dropped.

"Wow, that's a lot!" Her comment made me immediately doubt my decision. Erin is a girl who enjoys the finer things in life and isn't afraid to drop some dough.

*Was this too much?* My fierce inner money critic came out to play.

*This is too much. You need to spend less and save more because you know you will need that money for when bad things happen.*

But as I looked out at the glistening water with the dolphins swimming freely alongside the boat, I inhaled the crisp fresh air, knowing that I was at a crossroads. I had the money even though I didn't want to spend it. I knew I had to try something different. I didn't have any other choice but to hire her.

I returned to Columbus, Ohio, and felt a sigh of relief when I hugged my little people. There is always something about my husband that makes me feel safe and at home, which was exactly how I felt the moment I saw him. But the warm welcome home quickly turned into the 'Sunday scaries' as we began to prepare for the upcoming week.

I seamlessly jumped back onto my hamster wheel as the daily grind returned. That was, of course, until I received an offer to work full-time for a hip new company that had received awards for being one of the best places to work for women.

*This is it! It is the change I need. It is what I've been looking for!*

I did my market research and knew what I was worth. I stood firm in the number I asked for, which was almost double my current salary. The hiring manager went to bat for me, and I was giddy, thinking I was now going to be paid my worth! With the offer in hand, I debated whether to cancel my upcoming call with Mariko but decided to keep it.

*For once, I'll be in an environment where I can focus on just one business and be around people who are happy and excited to be at work! I'll have more time for family, and I can even start volunteering for their awesome causes.*

I had clear next steps, and I was excited for my next chapter to unfold. That is, until things got much worse.

**REFLECTIVE QUESTIONS**
- List one thing you can do to invest in yourself.
- Name five things you constantly think about but can't seem to find the time for or fail to do because it is outside of your comfort zone.
- Ask yourself, do other people notice that something seems off before I notice it within myself?

# CHAPTER 5

# UNCONSCIOUS DISCOVERIES

---

*"Working on our own consciousness is the most important thing that we are doing at any moment, and being love is a supreme creative act."*

RAM DASS

"Your job is not your purpose," Mariko stated.

I was finally on the phone with Mariko, the owner of Soul Priority, for our first official coaching call as she dropped this nuclear bomb.

It was a crisp fall afternoon, and it felt like ages since we last spoke. I had officially accepted a new job and was in a transition period. Mariko had given me specific instructions to find a quiet and comfortable place, and I couldn't think of anywhere better than my mom's house. Her backyard was surrounded by enchanting trees and was full of the calming feeling of being in nature. My mom had a fire burning in the cute little fire pit when I arrived.

There had always been something magical about the smell of a burning fire and being outside in nature, yet I spent the majority of my time indoors. With a journal and pen in my hand, I sat there anxiously waiting for Mariko's call.

My phone rang. "Hi, Lauren! Good to hear your voice again. I've been looking forward to our call. Do you feel settled and comfortable?"

"Hi, Mariko! Yes, I do! So how do you pronounce your name?"

"It's Ma-di-Ko. Thanks for asking. Shall we get started? I always ask my clients if they have a specific question or topic they want to address. Do you have any?"

"I do. I'd really like to focus on figuring out what I am passionate about and what my purpose is. I recently got a new job, and I am hopeful that it will be the one."

"Before we get started, I feel called to share that I am feeling a great deal of pain in your heart. From the outside, everything looks picture-perfect, but you have been conditioned to make life look pretty. The best way I can describe it is if you were given a multiple-choice question, you would always pick the answer that fits societal expectations versus the answer you want to pick. This is causing you to feel empty inside. This pain is preventing you from connecting with your soul and your purpose. Do you know where this pain may come from?"

"Ah . . . I am not really sure."

"Well, what's happened in your life that's been painful?"

I paused, realizing that I choose not to dwell on or think about painful things. I learned early on how to compartmentalize and put them in a box. If the box was opened, rarely was it coupled with emotion. Everything was just the facts.

"I guess it has been painful to watch my dad lose his ability to practice medicine in light of his brain tumor and mental health diagnosis. I hate seeing my mom struggling emotionally and financially. My brother struggles with substance abuse, which is really painful to watch and affects the family dynamic. My senior year of college was extremely challenging for more reasons than one. And sometimes, my husband, Brian, says things to me that I know he doesn't mean. It usually happens when we've been drinking, but it is still hurtful. We've been together since high school."

"Wow, that is a lot to unpack. You need to get to know Brian on a new and deeper level. Your youth has brought the two of you where you are today, but you've just been maintaining and you both need to incorporate more play. Your heart feels hurt, and you feel stuck because you want something deeper with him. I suggest figuring out who you want to be together, as individuals and as parents. How do you think the two of you could add more play into your life?"

"Oh gosh . . . I don't know," I admitted.

With excitement in her voice, she said, "What about going to see a comedian, wine tasting, dancing, or visiting an art museum?"

"We already do many of those things. We haven't tried dancing, but I don't think he would want to do that."

"I have a few clients who speak very highly of tantric sex."

*Sex.*

I heard the word and instantly knew my husband would entertain anything that involved sex! Like most men, he couldn't seem to get enough of it. I wrote down tantric sex in my journal as Mariko continued to talk.

"My clients tell me it helps them immerse themselves in the present moment. They tell me it helps to deepen their physical, emotional, and spiritual connection with their partner."

With a grin on my face, I said, "I'll be sure to look into that."

"I'll be honest, there is not a lot of time for play," I added. "Sometimes I just want someone to throw me out into the water so I can float on my raft in peace."

Mariko began to laugh. "That is because you are the rock. You need to learn how to become more flexible with yourself and others."

*Flexible? I'm always doing things and accommodating my schedule for others. How could I be more flexible?*

Then it hit me like a ton of bricks. I realized that when Mariko told me that I needed to learn how to be more flexible, she meant I needed to stop having harsh rules and expectations for myself and others—expectations that no human could live up to, which made life feel hard. She was talking about having flexibility with my black-and-white thinking and realizing there is more than one way to do something. I needed to add more color to my life.

"Lauren, your soul already knows what it wants since it is a part of you. More than likely, you're letting your ego take over."

*Is she speaking a different language? My ego? Do I even have an ego?*

Whenever I heard the word ego, I pictured a bulky body-builder who was really into themselves.

"You see, your soul and your ego are two very different things. Your soul is who you are; it is your blissful self, whereas your ego is who you think you are, who you think you *should* be. Our purpose is to grow into a higher state of consciousness closer to enlightenment with our soul—not our ego. Your ego will make you do things you don't want to do even if your soul knows what it wants. Our egos ensure that we continue our automatic habits—habits that are likely unconscious because those keep us safe."

*Unconscious habits, hm . . . I wonder what those are for me?*

Very bluntly, Mariko shared, "It feels as though all of your thoughts are negative. Statistics show that a person has over sixty thousand separate thoughts per day."

*Holy shit, I think she is right,* I thought as I watched the flames from the fire move from orange to blue.

It had never occurred to me what was going on upstairs in my mind. It was as if my thoughts were on cruise control, filled with anxiety and fueled by fear.

*Negative thoughts are running my life!*

"Would you mind sharing with me some of the thoughts you have each day?"

I didn't know where to start. The fire dimmed, and I threw in another log. "It's a long list," I admitted.

"Just start," Mariko said.

"Okay. I have thoughts like, I should have done that better. Why can't I have more self-control when it comes to food? It takes me twice as long to read and understand something compared to other people. I suck because I don't get to my whole to-do list. Why couldn't I be more patient with my kids? I am not smart enough to do that. My arms are too big. I don't have a creative bone in my body. There is no time to do anything I want to do."

"Lauren, these are all great examples of limiting beliefs. It is clear to me that you have not taken the time to celebrate who you are, what you have, or the things you have achieved. For God's sake, you went to law school and passed the bar the first time! Do you think this is something that everyone does?"

*Well, I am sure anyone could do it if they wanted to.*

"I want you to tell me that you went to law school and passed the bar."

Mariko forced me to press the pause button to acknowledge how far I had actually come. I began to have déjà vu of when my best friend forced me to tell two strangers we had met what I did for a living because I wouldn't share that I was an attorney.

*Why would I not tell people that I am an attorney?*

I realized that I was constantly trying to prove that I was good enough to be an attorney. I needed to perfect the art of being one before I could say it out loud. There wasn't time to celebrate wins because I was too busy proving myself.

*Wow! All of these achievements that I've ever wanted clearly are not bringing me the fulfillment and peace I thought they would.*

The hot dragon's breath of paying back $130,000 of law school debt prevented me from slowing down to focus on any of my achievements.

Mariko shared, "Despite your limiting beliefs, I want *you* to know that you are able to create anything you want in life."

I quickly responded in a soft voice, "Well, what if I don't know what I want?"

"Right now, your life is like *Groundhog Day*—constantly on repeat. You don't know what you want because you aren't going outside of your box. You're not going after your dreams."

*My dreams? I've achieved my dreams. What now?*

"What are your dreams?" Mariko asked.

There was a long pause followed by my infamous, "I don't know. I've achieved my dreams. I got married, we have healthy kids and a house, and we're financially stable."

"That's a beautiful foundation, but what do you really want now?"

"Brian and I really want to go to Italy and Greece for our ten-year anniversary, maybe buy a lake house and travel abroad with our kids. I also want to obtain a certification that would indicate I specialize in data privacy. Oh! I want to buy a boat, but boats don't make sense financially, living in Ohio. We could only use it like four months out of the year."

"Great!" She exclaimed. "See, you're onto something here. You just had to give yourself some space to come up with the answers. You know, you don't have to buy a boat to fulfill your dream. Why don't you look into renting a boat or lake house to get a feel for what it would be like?"

*Why didn't I think of this?* Her idea was so simple yet so profound.

"I'll be honest. It never dawned on me to just rent a boat, but I am going to look into this. I guess I always thought there would just be a good time to buy it, likely when I had cash to pay for it."

*Ah ha, I've had blinders on all along. My mind is only wired to see things one way: my way!*

Everything else seemed so urgent, which placed buying a boat low on the list of things to do.

*Hell, was there ever a right time? Why is work and my dad's stuff so urgent?*

I quickly wrote down, "STOP being paralyzed to act on what you DESIRE!"

"Ah, yes. Stress can get the best of us," Mariko admitted. "Do you know how to do a box breath or meditate?"

"No, I don't," I admitted.

"That's okay," she said. "Meditation and breathing are known to help reduce stress. I encourage you to incorporate them into your day. You don't have to spend a lot of time on it—just start. Let's try a box breath now."

I placed my notebook and pen in the grass and placed my phone in my lap on speaker.

"Sit up tall and relax your neck and shoulders. Open up your mouth just slightly and relax your tongue. I want you to take a deep breath in for five seconds, filling yourself up with air as your stomach begins to expand. Once you've taken in all of the air, hold your breath at the top for five seconds. Now, slowly begin to let out your air through your nose or mouth for the count of five. When you have completely exhaled, hold that empty space at the bottom of your belly for five seconds."

*Did I just do that right?*

"Repeat this as many times as you would like," she said. "I recommend starting to try this for five minutes each day and build off that. I also want you to know there are also so many wonderful natural Ayurvedic herbs and supplements that help combat stress and anxiety."

Our precious time was coming to an end, and while I was intrigued by the conversation, I became frustrated that we had barely talked about my job or career. After all, the whole reason why I hired her was to figure out what I was supposed to be doing with my life.

"Mariko, do you think we could shift to my job and career?"

"Certainly. Your job is not your purpose!" she exclaimed. "People think they are what they do, but that is not your purpose. Your purpose is to have fun, to do what inspires and is meaningful to you! You are here to connect people to each other and be of service to others. Life is about compassion and love and just doing the little things in life. Really, just embodying your true self is your purpose. Once you realize who you are, you can create from that."

I stopped taking notes.

*What the actual fuck. This is not helpful.*

"How could you use your law degree to be of service to others?" she asked. "Have you thought about working in a different setting or focusing on a different area of the law? What if you hosted or assisted with fundraisers or events that were heart-centered social justice issues that you cared about? You could do this outside of your day job, and you may find that it will bring fulfillment into your life."

"Yeah, maybe."

*In all my fucking spare time that I don't have.*

"I want you to remember that when you create or start something new, it doesn't mean that you are starting over."

*Phew! I really don't want to start over. I've worked so hard to get here.*

With desperation in my voice, I said, "I know we don't have much time left, and I still don't know what this missing feeling inside me is."

"You are forbidden from saying 'I don't know' *ever* again! You do know!" Mariko's voice was sharp, causing me to stop drawing random circles in my notes.

*Do I?*

"Let me ask you this," Mariko said. "What type of environment do you want to be in?"

"I want to be in a fun, flexible, and happy environment where I am afforded a work-life balance so that I am not stressed and anxious all of the time."

"Great! And what do you want to do?"

"I want to make the world a better place by helping people."

"Awesome! That is your missing link. You want to be happy while serving others. Lauren, you get to be *you*, and you get to sprinkle your fairy dust on everyone you meet."

*Is life really that easy? Surround yourself in an environment that suits you and show up as you?*

The sun was starting to go down, and it was beginning to get cold. I looked down at my watch and was shocked to see that four hours had passed.

"Well, I think it is time to wrap things up now. I will check in with you in a couple of weeks to see how you are doing."

"Thank you so much for your time, Mariko. I hope to report back that the new job is the perfect fit."

**REFLECTIVE QUESTIONS**

- List your top five achievements and then go celebrate!
- Write down at least ten painful things you've experienced in life.
- Identify three ways that you can add more fun, joy, and play into your life.

# CHAPTER 6

# HAMSTER WHEEL

———

*"Insanity is doing the same thing over and over and expecting different results."*

ALBERT EINSTEIN

A few months after the clarity call and starting my new job, I sat hunched over my knees on a Friday night in my closet, crying uncontrollably. I kept trying to catch my breath.

I was drinking from a fire hose at the new job that I had thought would be the perfect fit. Instead, it was making me physically weak and extremely emotional. My patience and strength had abandoned me, and other than ordering a tantric sex how-to video, I hadn't given any attention to my notes from my call with Mariko.

Each week was harder than the last. The closet breakdown week was kicked off with the 'Sunday scaries.' I felt worthless. I dreaded going to work the next morning.

The following morning, I was startled by the blaring alarm. I hit the snooze button and mindlessly started checking work emails with one eye open. Almost immediately, my body tensed, and my anxiety started to rise before I even stepped foot off the bed.

*Please make the emails stop!*

Halfway through responding to an email, I heard my daughter, Maya, crying in her crib. My feet hit the floor, and I was off to the races. Maya saw me, and her tears quickly turned into a smile as I pulled her out of the crib to change her diaper. As I watched her smile and coo, I saw the clock read 6:45 a.m. I was late. I had one hour to get everyone ready, drop the kids at day care, and drive downtown for a meeting.

As I clipped a small bow in Maya's hair, my son Brody made his way into her room and wrapped his little arms around my leg. In typical morning fashion, Brody jumped on my back, and I carried both kids downstairs for breakfast. The Keurig was calling my name, and so were the "I'm so hungry" squeals. Grabbing two frozen waffles, blankets, and their iPads, I managed to get the little people settled.

As I poured my cinnamon coffee, I assembled their lunches, backpacks, nap supplies, and water bottles. I raced back upstairs with fifteen minutes to get myself ready while I tried to enjoy my now-lukewarm coffee. I made my way back downstairs to find that Brody had only eaten a bite of his breakfast and refused to go upstairs.

"But Mom, I am not done yet. I don't want to go get ready," He cried.

"I'm sorry, but it's time to go to school. You can take your breakfast with you."

Brody stood up as I threw Maya on my hip. I had precisely six minutes to get Brody dressed, brush his teeth, and get jackets and shoes on, in addition to loading the forty pounds of their stuff into the car.

Brody began to cry, "I don't want to wear this! These jeans are too big."

*Someone fucking help me!*

Brody lay face down on the floor in protest. I heard my phone ding.

*Seriously, twenty-two new emails? I'm not even at work yet!*

I burst into tears and yelled, "Brody, please just help Mommy. Put your clothes on. Mommy has to get to work."

My alarming behavior snapped Brody out of his state. It was the first time either of my kids had seen me cry.

Brody peeled himself off the ground and sat down next to me. "Mommy, why are you sad? I am sorry if I upset you."

*Why am I crying right now? You don't have time to cry. Get it together!*

*Am I just tired?*

*Am I resentful at Brian because he couldn't help me with the kids this morning?*

*Am I mad that I have an early meeting that I don't want to go to?*

*Am I sad it was my fault that Brody couldn't finish his breakfast?*

*Do I just need to finish my coffee and eat something?*

"You didn't upset me, Brody. I am okay. Mommy just woke up on the wrong side of the bed, but it would really help Mommy if you put on your clothes."

*Thank you, Jesus; he's listening.*

As we were about to load up the car, I remembered Brody needed a family picture for a school project.

*Motherfucker. How did I forget this?*

I dropped the kids and their bags, ran to the basement, praying I wouldn't break my ankle on all of the toys, and grabbed the first picture I saw.

*Why is getting out the door so damn hard?*

It was as if I were running a marathon every morning—one of those Tough Mudder marathons where they tell you to climb over a wet forty-five-degree object with no rope.

My phone read 8:00 a.m.

*Great! I'm going to be late. There is no way I can drop the kids off and drive downtown in thirty minutes.*

Meanwhile, the peanut gallery was screaming, "Mommy, my buckle is too tight! Fix it!" But there was no time to fix anything.

*Phew, we made it.*

Day care drop off and the forty pounds of bags

I scurried the kids and their belongings into the school as I attempted to get into the building using their fingerprint keypad—access denied.

*What the fuck? Just let me in; these are my kids. Why is everything so hard!*

Just as I was feeling sorry for myself, the sweet director at the front desk saw me struggling and buzzed me in. We proceeded up the two flights of stairs and headed for Maya's classroom. I squeezed her goodbye and watched her run straight for the kitchen.

Brody and I walked across the hall to his room. "I hope you have a great day, buddy. I love you! We'll have some fun later tonight."

I kissed Brody goodbye. With the little people safe, happy, and out of my care, I felt lighter. Just as the sigh of relief came, so did a sweeping amount of guilt for my alarming behavior and having to rush them out of the house.

On my way out, the director stopped me. "Hey, we need you to fill out this form for Maya to ensure she is up to date with her shots. We need it by the end of the week."

I thanked her, grabbed the form, and sprinted to my car. As the car door shut, I burst into tears.

*Why am I crying again? She just handed you a piece of paper.*

Shame filled my body at the thought that I was too busy to make an appointment or take Maya to the doctor.

*You wanted this, Lauren. Remember when you couldn't even afford to send your kids here.*

There was no time to sulk because I was late. I sped down the freeway, praying that I wouldn't get pulled over as I called the pediatrician's office. Given my earlier outbursts, I knew I needed to course-correct, so I booked myself a facial.

*Surely a facial will make me feel better!*

I pulled into the parking garage and ran into the building.

*Phew. I'm only five minutes late. Bring on marathon number two.*

Like clockwork, I attended meeting after meeting. I even squeezed in a few emails while I peed in the bathroom. It wasn't long before I found myself cuddling on the couch with Brody and Maya, slamming a Costco-sized bag of Doritos. *Get off the couch; you need to prepare for tomorrow. No, I just need five more minutes.*

I finally made it to Friday, and every day seemed to be repeating itself. I had been working around the clock helping a team get a new product into the market. I was affording the business the best legal advice I could muster, but it never seemed to be enough. Given the product's complexities, I found myself on a 5:00 p.m. call with outside counsel. About thirty minutes into the call, a reminder popped up on my phone: "FACIAL 6:00 p.m."

*Shit!*

I quickly joined the call from my cell phone and began driving to the spa. Frustration started to build as I drove because the call was supposed to provide me with answers and insights I could share with the business. Yet the call was confusing me and diminishing my confidence because I wasn't able to follow the circular logic that was being presented.

*How am I going to be able to get the business an answer by Monday? Why can't I get this?*

Brian's call beeped in on the other line; I hit, "Sorry, I can't talk right now." I sat in the spa's parking lot, already ten minutes late. I wrapped up the call feeling worse than when I started it. My eyes began to swell with tears.

*Why do you care so much? It's Friday. You know you will be met with resistance no matter what you give the business. Go inside and enjoy your facial.*

As I lay on the warm bed, I tried my best to relax and get comfortable. I couldn't get out of my own head.

*What am I going to tell the business? If a prestigious law firm does not know, how am I supposed to have an answer?*

I continued to hear my phone vibrate, and the therapist asked me if I wanted her to stop, but I told her to keep going. Five minutes passed, and it dawned on me that Brian had tried to call me on my drive to the facial.

*Damn it! I forgot to tell him I had this facial. Not only do you suck at your job, but you suck at home too!*

The facial was over, and I had not even allowed myself to relax.

I flung on my clothes and grabbed my phone to read a text from Brian, "Are you planning to come home for dinner . . . Where are you?"

As I paid for the facial, I frantically called him to explain what happened. Within seconds, I could sense he was mad and frustrated as he said, "Again, Lauren, you need to communicate with me. I can't read minds. We'll see ya when we see ya; don't worry about us."

My heart sank.

*Did he seriously just hang up on me? Does he not realize how hard I'm trying here?*

I drove home, desperate to feel better and make Brian understand yet too exhausted to even try. I walked in the door, and the kids ran up and wrapped their little arms around my legs. I took a deep breath and let out a sigh as I dropped my bags.

Brian looked straight at me, "Wow, nice to finally see you. Am I supposed to just read your mind? I know you're busy, Lauren, but we are all busy, and I need you to communicate with me."

*He's right. I've completely shut down. When is the last time I even acknowledged him? Please just come and give me a hug and tell me it's going to be okay.*

"I understand you're frustrated with me, babe, but can you please just cut me a break. You know you guys are my whole world," I pleaded.

We stood in the kitchen as the kids played happily outside.

"Yup, it's your world, and we're just living in it."

His comment felt like a dagger penetrating my heart.

*Deep breath, Lauren. You know he is tired too, but where is he coming from?*

Furious and distraught by his comment, I shut down. I knew whatever came out of my mouth wouldn't be what he wanted to hear.

*Can't you see the invisible load I'm trying to carry? Can't you see what I am doing for our family? Do you think the clean clothes, food, cleaning, kids' activities, birthday gifts, bills, and homemade lunches get taken care of by some magic fairy?*

Feeling heartbroken, I sprinted upstairs to my closet.

There I sat, hunched over my knees, hands covering my face as tears uncontrollably poured out.

*Why does it feel like ten people are sitting on me? What the fuck am I doing? Why can't I seem to get off this hamster wheel? Is it this hard to give my kids the life I had growing up? Why do I continue to think that a new job or external things will make me feel better?*

Before I could finish the thought, the closet door opened slowly. I prayed it was Brian headed in to comfort me.

Instead, I was greeted by Brody.

*Don't let him see you like this.*

I wiped the tears from my face. With a soft voice, Brody asked, "Are you okay, Mommy?" as he placed his small hand on my back.

I tried to fight back the tears, but his pure words and gentle touch penetrated my being.

He wrapped his little arms around me and said, "It is okay to be sad, Mommy."

It was one of the first times when I was forced to sit with my feelings. There was nowhere to go and nothing to do. There were no distractions in sight.

**REFLECTIVE QUESTIONS**

- Name three things that make it difficult to get off the hamster wheel.
- Are the things you're doing in your life actually what you want now?
- Where in your life do you continue to do the same thing over and over again while expecting a different result?

# CHAPTER 7

# THE PRACTICE

---

*"The past has no power over the present moment."*

ECKHART TOLLE

My colleague looked me dead in my eyes and, with genuine concern, asked, "Are you okay?"

It was only a week after my closet breakdown that I walked out of an important meeting. Not only was I the lead in this meeting, but I was also tasked with researching and drafting a paramount memo that was needed by the end of the day.

*There is no way I can pull this off.*

My anxiety skyrocketed. I had no idea where to begin. My brain was shutting down from sheer overload. I found an open office and forcefully shut the door. I immediately burst into tears. My chest was tight, and I couldn't catch my breath. I was boxed into the small office surrounded by four white walls, praying nobody would walk in. I felt helpless. I was desperate to find a way out.

*I need to quit. I just need to quit. Get it together, Lauren. You're at work. You can't quit! You haven't even been here a year.*

Unable to catch my breath, I heard Mariko's voice.

*A box breath helps to relieve stress by breathing deeply.*

I fixated my eyes on the word "data" written on the dry-erase board that hung on the wall.

*Breathe in. One, two, three, four, five.*

*Hold your breath. One, two, three, four, five.*

*Now let everything go. One, two, three, four, five.*

*Now hold your breath. One, two, three, four, five.*

Slowly, I could feel my breath starting to regulate itself, and the tears began to let up.

"This too shall pass," I began to whisper.

*Why are these breakdowns getting more intense? This can't be happening at work.*

I knew if I wanted something to change, not only did I have to do something differently, but the change needed to be something I did consistently.

*Did I really think that one intense life coaching session would make everything better?*

As I left work that day, a colleague said, "Looking forward to seeing you and your husband at the Christmas party this weekend."

*The Christmas party. Don't forget to buy a dress.*

With babysitters secured, we found ourselves at the Art Institute. It was open and spacious and glittering with magnificence as my husband and I walked up the stairs dressed in our formal attire. This was my first formal company holiday party, and I was in absolute awe of the gourmet food, elaborate drinks, live bands, laughter, and all the extra bells and whistles.

*Why aren't you on cloud nine? You've been dying to be invited to a Christmas party just like this one!*

As I stood in a crowded room next to my husband, I began talking to my coworker's wife. "Hi, I don't think we've met before. My name is Lauren."

I couldn't help but notice her tall, lean stature; her broad, sturdy shoulders; and her defined jawline as she stood there with such poise.

"Hi, I am Stacie, Ben's wife."

"Ben! I love your husband; he helped me get a job here. Tell me more about you. Do you work outside of the home?"

"Yes, I do," she said. "I am a yoga teacher at an academy here in town. I teach younger students and also teach private lessons."

She told me she had been teaching for four years and practicing for fifteen. I felt my heart beat faster.

"I've been thinking about trying yoga, but I'm hesitant to go to a studio because I have no idea what the heck I'm doing. Something tells me I could benefit from it, though. Would you be willing to do a private lesson with me?" I asked.

*Did you seriously just ask her for a private lesson? You don't even know her! You have jumped off the deep end, Lauren.*

I stood there anxiously waiting for her to respond as I thought about my former colleague telling me years prior to consider yoga. I had laughed at her and brushed her off by telling her that if I had an extra hour to kill, you wouldn't find me burning fifty calories at a yoga class.

Stacie smiled and said, "Sure. I'd be happy to introduce you to the practice."

*The practice? Wasn't this just yoga? What the hell did I just sign up for?*

The next morning, I picked up my phone and texted Stacie. I couldn't believe I was following through, but something inside me believed yoga could help.

It wasn't long before I found myself sitting on a yoga mat with Stacie sitting six feet across from me.

Stacie asked, "So tell me, what brought you here today?"

I froze and couldn't speak. My eyes started to fill with tears. Without uttering a word, Stacie patiently waited for me to speak as she sat up tall with her hands resting on her knees. It felt so uncomfortable sitting across from someone that I didn't even know—not to mention that I was about to try something new and foreign.

"I'm not exactly sure," I said as I wiped my tears with my hand. "I am constantly stressed with work, and I don't feel like myself. It is starting to take a toll on me and my family.

I looked down at the wood floor and admitted, "I can't seem to enjoy my life. Even during times that I should feel happy, like my son's birthday party, I constantly feel like I am pushing through everything, checking a box, going through the motions, and waiting for the other shoe to drop."

"You are not alone in your feelings," she said. "I, too, have felt this and continue to question and push back on societal demands. Yoga helps me press the pause button and stay in the present moment. Oftentimes, we are looking too far ahead, which causes anxiety, while dwelling in the past can cause depression or sadness. Start to ask yourself, 'What is it that I am feeling now? What is it that I need in this moment?'"

"Let's stand up and start moving our bodies. Stand tall and feel your spine lengthen. Feel the space you are creating for yourself. Unlock your knees and give them a little bend. Now roll your hips under and activate your pelvic floor by drawing in your muscles in your lower abdomen by squeezing them up."

"Keep your butt and legs relaxed," she said. "Release the tension in your shoulders, neck, and jaw by slightly opening up your mouth. This is a proper standing position. Can you feel how relaxed, sturdy, and aware you are in this position? Do you feel your connection with the Earth and its grounding sensation? Can you feel your power in this neutral stance?"

*This feels so awkward.*

"This may feel foreign because your body is not used to standing in its natural position."

*Is she reading my mind?*

"Now place your right hand over your heart and your left hand over your belly. I want you to take a deep breath in, filling up with air starting from the bottom of your belly. Slowly feel your belly fill up with air. Pretend you are smelling a beautiful flower, smelling it slow and steady. Can you feel your chest expanding? Now slowly let out your breath through your mouth. Let's do this three more times," she instructed.

With each inhale and exhale, I felt calm, with a hint of power, standing in this strong, grounded position.

For the next hour, Stacie guided me through a number of yoga poses like downward dog, warrior one, warrior two, and tree pose.

*This isn't so hard.*

"You are doing awesome! Now we get to move to what I like to call the dessert of yoga, savasana. Lie on your back and get into a comfortable position. Now close your eyes and let your body and mind be still in relaxation. Just allow yourself to *be* in this present moment. Don't judge whatever comes up. Just notice and be here. Let whatever thoughts you are having come and go as if they were trickling down a calm river."

As I allowed my mind and body to relax, I continued to focus on my breathing. Slow and steady, in and out. Savasana was soothing. There was nothing to do and nowhere to be.

"Now I want you to start waking up your body by turning to your right side. Don't rush it; just allow your body to transition slowly. Great! Now sit up and meet me in a seated position."

Stacie took her hands and held them together slightly above her eyes as if she were praying and said, "The light in me honors the light in you. Namaste."

Stacie asked me how I felt.

"I certainly feel more relaxed and grounded. It was easy to follow your instructions and wasn't as intimidating as I thought. I had no idea that my posture was so poor and that I was only breathing in through my chest. I can really tell the difference when I breathe deeply."

"Yes, most people don't notice their breathing is shallow, but there are extreme benefits from taking full breaths. You should look into what yoga studios are in your area and think about practicing. I think you would notice a big difference in your day-to-day if you incorporated a class into your busy schedule."

As we put away our mats, I looked down at my phone and was shocked to see that two hours had passed.

*I gotta get home; Maya has music class soon.*

Each Saturday, six toddlers and their parents sit in a circle and sing, dance, and play with instruments as we follow the teachers' instructions. This Saturday was no different.

Maya sat patiently on my lap with a big smile as she waited for the teacher to start class.

"Hi, friends! Let's start today's class by singing 'This Little Light of Mine' as we clap our hands to the beat. Parents, you sing along too!"

With her beautiful, loud voice, the teacher started singing. "This little light of mine, I'm going to let it shine. This little light of mine, I'm going to let it shine. Come on, parents, don't be shy," the teacher said as she clapped her hands to the song.

As I watched Maya parade around the room so freely, I began to hear my own faint voice sing, "This little light of mine. I'm going to let it shine."

My eyes started filling with tears.

*Where is my light? Where did it go?*

I quickly wiped my tears so that nobody would see that I was crying. It was too painful to sing, and I knew if I continued, I wouldn't be able to hold back the flood of tears. As the rest of the class continued, I grabbed Maya and told her teacher I wasn't feeling well.

*Why am I having breakdown after breakdown? The only thing you have been practicing is crying. You need to find a new practice, Lauren.*

Desperate for answers, the only thing I could think to do was call Mariko.

**REFLECTIVE QUESTIONS**

- Name the last time you tried something new that felt foreign.
- Are you able to fully immerse yourself in the present moment and enjoy your experience?
- Name two bodily triggers that you notice when you are stressed.

**GROWTH EXERCISE**

- Dr. Joe Dispenza found that when you squeeze your pelvic floor, it starts to rewire your brain by secreting spinal fluid that travels up your spine. That fluid hits the pineal gland and sends the brain signals to trigger a balanced response in the body. Watch his free YouTube video titled: "Pineal Gland Awakening with Dr. Joe Dispenza | How to Upgrade Your Brain."

## CHAPTER 8

# BREAKDOWNS LEAD TO BREAKTHROUGHS

———

*"I find myself only by losing myself."*

PAUL RICOEUR

As I was lying in a fetal position on the floor of my daughter's bedroom, Mariko, the owner of Soul Priority, listened to me cry hysterically on the other end of the phone.

"Take a deep breath and tell me what has been going on since we last spoke," Mariko said.

I tried to catch my breath.

"Ever since our intensive clarity call, my life feels even worse. I don't understand why since our call helped me realize so many things. My feelings have never felt this intense in my entire life, and they are too much for me to handle. I break down and cry all the time. I'm questioning everything I thought I ever wanted. I can't handle the stress anymore. I think I need to quit my job."

*You have officially lost it, Lauren!*

Suddenly, my absolute worst fear of not being able to provide for my family or sustain myself was the direction I wanted to head. I felt trapped. I couldn't see any way out other than quitting, even though I didn't have another job to go to. "I don't think you need to make such a drastic move. And let me remind you that you opened the floodgates to all of these feelings that you have been suppressing. When you called me, you decided to open up those gates. Now that they are open, they can't be shut. You must work through what you're feeling."

*Surely there is a way I can shut these gates!*

"I think I need anti-anxiety meds to help me through this."

Her voice softened, "You may, but there are also great natural Ayurvedic supplements out there that we discussed during your clarity call. Do you have the notes from our call?"

"Yes, I have them right here."

*Why haven't I looked at these or done anything with them?*

"Take your paper and pen and write this down. 'I ground myself in my awareness that I am a spiritual being. I am whole, I am complete, I am an instrument of divine light and love.' That just came from you and it's beautiful!"

*What the hell? There is no way this just came from me.*

I sat there staring blankly at the piece of paper, feeling shattered in every way. I was anything but whole and complete.

"I want you to use this affirmation each morning before you do anything else. Set a timer on your phone for five minutes and repeat it until the timer goes off."

I hung up the phone and knew there was no way an affirmation or supplements would work. My heart beat faster as my panic and anxiety hit in waves. I dialed my doctor's office and pleaded with the nurse for anti-anxiety medication.

When the nurse said the doctor would call a prescription into the pharmacy, my body relaxed and a sense of relief washed over me. I drove to the pharmacy as soon as I could.

"Sorry! We are closed!" read the sign.

*No, please, no—closed!*

It was too late to get the prescription transferred. I had about two hours of work to do, but there was nothing left in me. I hit an official breaking point and didn't even care about the work I was supposed to do. I lay helplessly on my bed, eyes swollen, feeling empty, as I drifted off to sleep. I later learned from a spiritual teacher that this specific evening was the dark night of my soul when my old self died and my new self was born. The next morning, I naturally woke up without an alarm. My family was still sleeping. I couldn't recall the last time I had woken up without an alarm. I felt strangely calm.

*Did I get the sleep that I needed? Maybe I cried so hard that I just got everything out of me?*

With the pharmacy still closed and a strong desire for change, I didn't have a choice but to try the affirmation Mariko had told me to write down. I grabbed a blanket and my notebook and headed to my formal living room. My awakening process was underway. The expansive ceilings and large windows gave me a view of the trees planted in our backyard. The sky was still dark. I sat down right in front of the windows, wrapped a blanket around my shoulders, and set the alarm on my phone for five minutes. I began reading the affirmation written in my journal over and over again.

*I ground myself in my awareness that I am a spiritual being. I am whole. I am complete. I am an instrument of divine light and love.*

As each minute passed, I allowed the words to sink in as they began to resonate. My timer buzzed. When I finished, I was shocked by how grounded I felt and how good it felt to let those words sink into my body.

How could strange words on a piece of paper make me feel like this?

I realized I had lost my faith, and those words reminded me that I was part of something larger than myself. They reminded me that I was a spiritual being.

I made a big decision at that moment. I decided not to pick up my anti-anxiety medication. I remembered my mom having trouble getting off her medications, and I didn't want to have those troubles. But most importantly, I could feel the calmness and power within me.

*I am not going to be the victim of a job. I am not going to let a job control my life. My job will not be the reason why I get on medication.*

Little did I know, my work was not the sole cause of the plethora of emotions I was experiencing. Rather, it was a lifetime's worth of stuffed feelings and fears that were surfacing. I read through the notes I had taken months earlier during my clarity call with Mariko. I wrote four action steps:

1. Repeat affirmation for five minutes each morning.
2. Text Mariko and order her recommended supplements.
3. Purchase *No Matter What* by Lisa Nichols on Audible and listen to the book while driving to work.
4. Have fun with Brian! Set time aside to learn and try tantric sex.

Every day, no matter what, my five minutes of sacred time became nonnegotiable.

Ironically, the first week I started, Patricia, a sister of a college roommate, mailed me a small book filled with daily devotions called *Jesus Calling*. Patricia's thoughtful and needed gesture came shortly after a birthday celebration dinner for her sister, where I shared that I wasn't doing well. Normally, I found people who pushed their faith onto other people offensive, but this gracious act felt different. As I continued to do my affirmation each morning, I began incorporating a short daily passage from *Jesus Calling*.

Each morning, I felt mentally and physically stronger. I allowed the words that I am *whole* and *complete* to sink in. I no longer needed to read my affirmation from the piece of paper. I had it memorized. I began saying it out loud. The first time I said it, my voice was faint. It reminded me of the time I heard my voice singing "This Little Light of Mine" at Maya's music class. Each time I forced myself to say it out loud, not only did it get me more comfortable using and hearing my own voice, but I also began to hear my own confidence and authority.

My morning affirmation practice quickly expanded throughout my entire day. If I felt myself getting stressed or anxious, I would pause for a deep breath in as I repeated my affirmation.

*I ground myself in my awareness that I am a spiritual being. I am whole. I am complete. I am an instrument of divine light and love.*

My boss confirmed what I already knew by sharing that I seemed happier. The affirmation helped to shift me back into the present moment and reminded me of who I really am.

*I am an instrument of divine light and love.*

My actions started to mirror my inside growth as I started to take the time to smile and see people as they walked past me. I started sending birthday cards, something I always thought about doing but never made the time for. I repeated my affirmation so many times that it became ingrained in me. You would have thought these were my first words out of the womb.

Instead of crying in the car each morning and making calls to people that drained me, I listened to *No Matter What* by Lisa Nichols. Her powerhouse voice and story restored strength and hope in me. I began to have faith that I had the power within me to change and was supported by a higher power than myself. Brian and I even made time to watch the "how-to" tantric sex video. Let's just say it was the 1980s version and we were dying with laughter. It forced us to lock eyes for a long period of time, and when it was all said and done, I was crying with tears of laughter and deep joy.

*You're making progress. Keep going!*

**REFLECTIVE QUESTIONS**
- Name one major breakdown in your life. What breakthrough did you have from it?
- Do you trust in a higher power, or have you lost your faith?
- What can you do today that will help you move in a direction you'd like to go?

**GROWTH EXERCISE**
- Create your own "I AM" affirmation by going to mindmusclemotivator.com.

## CHAPTER 9

# TRUST THE PROCESS

———

*"Nothing goes away until it has taught us what we need to know."*

PEMA CHODRON

*I am finally going to do it! I am going to execute my worst fear and quit my job without having another job to go to.*

After months and months of stress, questioning my life and starting to acknowledge what I actually wanted, I decided I would rely solely upon my husband to support our family.

*Geeze, I can't believe I'm about to give up something I've worked so hard for. Am I sure I'm ready to give up over $200,000?*

I couldn't believe I was going to explore quitting my job. I knew I needed to be in control of my family's security and my own financial independence. I hated to disappoint anyone, and I had not even made it a year into the job.

*You really shouldn't quit a job you just started. It will look bad on your resume.*

Yet something inside told me to trust the loud voice inside of me that was now yelling at me.

*Everything will be okay. You will figure this out.*

I began crunching numbers, calling our financial advisor, and strategizing different scenarios before presenting the options to Brian.

With calculated options in hand, I approached Brian. "Babe, I know this is going to sound crazy, but I need to quit my job. I just can't do it anymore. The money is great, but it's not worth the stress on our family or my mental health."

He looked at me with a blank stare as if he didn't know me or what words were coming out of my mouth.

"I have no idea what I am going to do, but I can take the kids out of day care and stay home with them," I said.

*He'll love this option! He's always wanted me to stay home with the kids.*

He took a step closer and hugged me. "You know what the right answer is. I trust you. You know I'll support you in whatever you decide, but I want you to think about this a little more. Why don't you wait until we do that training we signed up for a month ago before you make any decisions?"

The training was a two-part emotional intelligence leadership retreat split over two weekends. It was a total commitment of seven twelve-hour days. Schlaine, my colleague who recommended the program to me, suggested I take Brian to an introductory meeting so we could gain insights into the transformational program. Unexpectedly, Brian decided to sign up with me.

"The training is only two weeks away," he said.

*I can't wait that long!*

"I don't want you to take this the wrong way, but do you really think you'll be happy staying home with the kids all day? Plus, the kids thrive in day care."

*Fuck, he's right. Be honest with yourself, Lauren. You made peace with yourself a long time ago that you were not meant to stay home with the kids.*

I was grateful he pointed out what I already knew, but I couldn't think of another way out. I also couldn't justify the $2,300 dollar-a-month day care bill if I was sitting at home without a job.

*You'll figure it out, Lauren. Just keep going. The training is only a couple of weeks away.*

Stewing on what I should do about my job, I submersed my body in the hot lavender-salted water and sent a text to a senior vice president, telling her I didn't think I could keep doing this work. I thought she could provide some insight. She quickly responded, telling me that I could and that if I was uncomfortable, it was a good thing because it meant I was growing. I was intrigued. I had never heard this before. I was indeed uncomfortable.

*What am I growing into?*

I realized that I was growing into someone who was honoring their desires. That evening, I wrote my resignation letter. The next day, I called my boss in Atlanta to let him know that I had decided it was best if I quit. At first, he thought I was kidding and started joking that I had kids to pay for and needed money to get my nails done. But he heard the despair in my voice and asked whether I could hang on for a few more weeks while he investigated some potential options for me and the company. I obliged since I was still sorting things out with the financial advisor and waiting to attend the training.

*Time to get comfortable with the uncomfortable!*

While my boss investigated, Brian and I found ourselves driving to a training center located in the middle of a strip mall close to the high school we had graduated from. We stood awkwardly and nervously in a large, training room filled with more than one hundred strangers. I tried my best to be patient as my mind raced with anticipation. I was dying to know what we would be doing. Schlaine, who had completed the program herself, advised that the best thing we could do was to stay open to the program's possibilities. It reminded me of a quote I once saw by the Dalai Lama: "The mind is like a parachute. It works best when it is open."

At 9:00 a.m. sharp, we were ushered into a hallway as we prepared to enter the main training room.

The doors opened and we heard, "Welcome! Welcome! Everyone come in and quickly find a seat."

With everyone seated, the trainer introduced himself.

The trainer was full of energy and commanded the room's attention. After sharing pieces of his personal story and what we could expect for the weekend, he instructed us to stand up, giving us thirty seconds to find someone that we didn't know. He encouraged us to seek out someone that we wouldn't typically interact with.

I jumped out of my seat, and within seconds, I bumped into a Black woman wearing overalls, a bright pink shirt, and a cowgirl hat. She couldn't stop laughing and pointed out that based on our looks, we couldn't be more different. We then found out we would be partners for the first portion of the training.

The trainer instructed each of us to give our partner our full attention. We quickly locked eyes, and the room fell silent as we waited for further instructions.

*My god, this is uncomfortable! How much longer do we have to do this?*

I quickly realized the program's website was not lying when they said it would be experiential. As we continued to make eye contact, my mind raced. I couldn't recall the last time I made eye contact with someone. I was so busy running around like a wild maniac and trying to stay five steps ahead that I failed to notice anything directly in front of me.

On the second day of training, the trainer asked us to share with our partner all the things that we found ourselves doing daily. As I shared my list, she kindly reminded me that I mentioned packing my kids' lunches for school twice. *Well, those lunches are a bitch!*

As we continued to share, it became evident that there were several things we didn't like doing. The trainer asked us to participate in a reframing exercise utilizing the exact list that we previously shared with our partner. I found myself saying, "I get to prep and pack my kids' lunches every day," which was then followed by the hundred other things that I also get to do.

The reframing exercise was a simple, yet powerful, technique that served as a reminder that I am healthy and capable of doing things that others can't. It also made me realize that if I didn't like something, I could always choose something different. While some things didn't feel like a choice, like sending my kids to school without food, I realized I could have switched them to a different day care that provided lunches. The phrase, "Whatever you are not changing, you are choosing," became my new favorite mantra.

We continued to participate in various exercises such as answering journaling prompts, playing games, sharing with other people, and dancing, along with powerful visualizations that included screaming. Each one was designed for a specific purpose, but the entire program was created to blow up your typical day. It afforded each person sacred time to observe themselves and reflect on how they showed up in life, along with the opportunity to heal from past wounds and experiences.

On our way home each night, Brian and I would share our individual experiences. We quickly realized that each of us was having a very different emotional experience based upon who we were and our life experiences. We agreed that each exercise required a sense of trust since you never knew what was coming next. This sense of trust began to build a new muscle in my brain that forced me to relinquish control. As each exercise unfolded, I practiced letting go and having faith that each activity was exactly what I needed, when I needed it.

One guided visualization, where we were led to confront our own mortality, stuck with me and served as a powerful catalyst for change. As I sat in the dark, quiet training room, the visualization began as a lighthearted event, which quickly took an emotional turn. The trainer's detailed cues made me contemplate what regrets I had and how I'd be remembered. I couldn't help but think of what my sister once told me about me being good at getting shit done.

*Was the shit I did worthwhile? Is what I am doing making a difference in people's lives? Do I value the shit I'm doing?*

My answer, I realized, was a hard "no." Sure, there were days when I felt like I helped someone in the business or kept a family member from doing something stupid, but overall, I was running around like a madwoman. The visualization forced me to confront that I was my own worst enemy, that

I had lost sight of the most important things in my life, and that I had failed to act on my actual desires.

Tears streamed down my face at the thought of not being with my family. I felt miserable knowing that I gave more attention to issues at work that caused me stress and anxiety rather than spending time outside with my family and helping others. All I could think about was if I loved the people around me hard enough and whether I made enough time for the important things in life, like having compassion and letting those around me know how much I care about them.

I didn't want to be remembered as the person who complained all the time and was held down by her situation. Rather, I wanted to be remembered as a source of strength. A woman who lived with intention and passion. I didn't want to be remembered as the woman who was so hard on herself that she held herself back from living her true greatness. While I thought about the dysfunction in my family, my heart instantly filled with so much gratitude for them.

One of the final exercises left an imprint on my soul. The trainer carefully placed each person into small groups. Each group was given a specific mission that they would execute in front of the larger group. My group was composed of six other women who get shit done.

*Was I placed in this group on purpose? Is it a coincidence that we are all so similar?*

I couldn't help but notice that our group was given vague instructions compared to the other groups. My group looked at each other confused because the other groups had specific personas and performance assignments. I quickly raised my hand for more details. I needed to know what we would be expected to do. The trainer gave me a big smile and offered no further details.

*What the hell! We don't get to prepare like the other groups?*
*Tell me what we are supposed to do!*
We had several hours to kill before we were required to
return to the training room. As we drove away to shop for
outfits, my group began to laugh at the fact that we were all
overanalyzing what we would be asked to do. It was killing
each one of us that we had no control over the situation. We
quickly realized that our lesson was to *trust the process* and
learn how to enjoy ourselves in the present moment without
the need to know what was coming next. There was nothing
to plan or control. We just had to show up.

When we returned to the training center, we were
informed that our group would be the last to perform. It
was a test of whether I could enjoy the other groups' performances without getting in my head, continuously thinking
about what we would be asked to do without any time to
prepare. To my surprise, the performances were so capti-
vating that I lost myself in each one, especially my husband,
who was demonstrating a side of himself that I had never
seen before. It was so freeing to lose myself and enjoy the
present moment.

My group's turn quickly approached. The lights grew dim,
and the trainer turned off his microphone and asked us to
circle around him at the front of the room so he could explain
our mission. He told us that we are a special group who
observes everything around us and that we provide comfort
to others. Our assignment was a creative act of service that
required each woman to demonstrate in a vulnerable manner
our own internal light that had been reignited by the program while simultaneously giving to two other people who
also participated in the training.

The evening I performed my training assignment

This mission was the first time I experienced firsthand how my mind, body, and spirit could feel when I stopped resisting my need for control and my need to over-prepare. It was an "aha" moment that when I failed to trust the process, I willingly gave my power away because it exerted way more energy and drained the light within me. I didn't find it ironic that the areas in my life that I felt the most resistance and need for control were my greatest areas for growth.

While quitting my job was still on the table, the two weekend training sessions allowed me to look at my life and my job through a lens of opportunity and gratitude. My home became a fertile playing ground for fun and lightheartedness. Our family began having dance parties as we got ready in the morning, and we added zest into our week by planning something fun to look forward to during the week. There was no need to wait for the weekend anymore.

My stressful job afforded me the exact boot camp I needed to not only practice strict boundaries, but to step into my confident power, without the need to over-prepare. Deep down, I knew if I wanted lasting change, I needed to train every day and show up for myself based on what I desired. No longer would I allow fear to run my life. I focused on what I was getting done versus what wasn't. I began training my mind to stay in the present moment so that my mind was no longer focusing on the "what ifs."

As I continued to stand in my power, I witnessed my true authentic self emerging. I was no longer letting my mind feed the fears. Colleagues noticed I was using my voice more. A female friend told me she heard a calm firmness in my voice when I spoke or provided advice. I realized that the job I wanted to quit was perfectly placed in my path so I would hit rock bottom and grow. It taught me that jumping from job to job would not fix anything until I healed myself by addressing my fears, anxiety, and imposter syndrome.

These trainings instilled in me that I could trust the process of life, my own intuition, and the inner knowing that I have everything I need within me. No longer did I have a sense of urgency since I was cultivating patience for myself and others. Each day, I trained my mind that work could wait, and I got used to asking myself, "What do I need in this moment in order to give freely to those around me?"

No longer was I neglecting my body because there wasn't any time to work out. My outdoor lunch break runs became nonnegotiable. As I ran along the water ravine, I thought about who I was becoming—a passionate, powerful, present, and peaceful leader.

*A leader! This is so crazy considering I always wanted to be told what to do at work.*

Each time I thought about who I was becoming and the limitless possibilities that life offered, I'd feel a tingling sensation run up and down my body. I took it as a sign that I was on the right path. Just like the water running down the stream beside me, I was flowing with life. My resistance had dissipated. I still didn't know whether I would quit my job or whether something else would present itself, but I was becoming a master at relinquishing control and trusting the process of life, knowing I was exactly where I needed to be. It felt spectacular to be reconnected to myself and those around me.

**REFLECTIVE QUESTIONS**
- List your top three fears that keep you from trusting the process of life.
- Name the last time you felt outside of your comfort zone.
- What does trusting the process look like for you?

# CHAPTER 10

# NO YOU DID NOT

———

*"It takes humility to seek feedback. It takes wisdom to under-stand it, analyze it, and appropriately act on it."*

STEPHEN COVEY

My phone buzzed, and from the corner of my eye, I saw part of a text coming through from Schlaine that read "Angry... so so angry" and "inauthentic relationships."

*No, she did not!*

I was getting ready to attend another day of the emotional intelligence leadership training, and her text shook me to my core. The prior evening, the facilitator suggested we reach out to at least three people and request their feedback about what they thought was working in our life and what was holding us back. Outside of my annual work reviews, I realized I had never actively sought out feedback about myself. I was nervous about participating in this exercise and curious about the type of feedback I would receive.

I was strategic in who I asked to ensure I incorporated people who had known me for a while, those that didn't really know me, and those who only knew me in a work setting.

I texted my younger sister who experiences our family dynamic, my best friend from high school who I talk to daily, my brother since I was hard on him for his life choices, my colleague Schlaine who had only known me for six months, and an old colleague who I knew would give it to me straight. Their feedback was enlightening. It gave me the opportunity to fully comprehend my strengths, some of which I failed to acknowledge about myself. Since strengths come so naturally to us, I realized that it can be difficult to see them in ourselves. Each person had a consistent message based on what was working in my life. Feedback ranged from my natural leadership skills, determination, and thoughtfulness.

*Natural leadership skills? Me?*

All of the feedback, especially the negative, forced me to confront some hard truths. My brother told me that I could be very judgmental, black and white, and rigid, while my sister noted I could improve on being fully present. I received feedback from others attending the training that I overcomplicate things. Their feedback didn't shock my system like Schlaine's feedback about me being angry and inauthentic. Schlaine's feedback was raw and made me feel exposed.

*Why did the most valuable piece of feedback come from the person who has known me the least?*

Perhaps it was because Schlaine and I didn't have deep ties and she was able to offer an objective perspective. Or perhaps having undergone the training, she knew firsthand how powerful the exercise could be and didn't hold back because of it. It became apparent that those closest to me had a more difficult time sharing negative feedback with me.

I kept coming back to Schlaine's text.

*Inauthentic relationships? What did that even mean?*

I couldn't wrap my mind around it, so I asked her to elaborate. She felt that I was not being authentic to who I was, failed to honor my true feelings, and wore a mask to please others, which kept me from being fulfilled.

*Why couldn't I honor my true feelings? Was I really angry? Me, the put-together girl who never raises her voice and always has a big smile on her face?*

My best friend laughed when I shared this piece of feedback with her.

"Lauren, you know that is not true."

My emotions felt like they were on the biggest and fastest roller coaster in the amusement park. The more I ruminated, I began to accept that deep down, I was angry. I was angry that my dad got a brain tumor, which served as a catalyst that changed my childhood and unconsciously affected how I made decisions in my adult life. I was angry that the medical board forced him to give up his true passion for helping others as a doctor. I was angry to be the one tasked with managing his bipolar disorder that left me on wild goose chases and dealing with a broken health care system.

It pained me that my dad's brain tumor exacerbated things so significantly that my mom divorced him, yielding financial tension within the family. I was angry that my brother fell prey to the drug epidemic, which added additional stress to our family dynamic. I was angry and filled with feelings of absolute rage that nothing was done after a friend's boyfriend sexually assaulted me and another woman. Just acknowledging my anger and allowing myself to feel it helped me move through it.

After the hour screaming exercise and being called the "Ice Queen" in the training, I realized that I had learned how to suppress my anger and dissociate from my feelings as a coping mechanism because it was too painful to feel. I had a hard time feeling anything. I brushed everything under the rug and pushed on because it's not normalized to be angry or talk about mental illness. Schlaine's feedback unlocked a door—a door that needed to be open for me to explore, acknowledge, and process events and feelings so that I could become free from it all.

I noticed that when I received the negative feedback, my mind instinctively rationalized why it was not true. Receiving and processing feedback was hard! But I saw firsthand how necessary it was in order to grow and fully tap into my power. I considered myself to be a self-aware person, but some of my requested feedback blindsided me. Apparently, I wasn't alone in believing I was self-aware. Tasha Eurich, an organizational psychologist, conducted research on self-awareness and found that even though most people *believe* they are self-aware, self-awareness is a truly rare quality. I've found that self-awareness is the vehicle that allows our passions and purpose to discover us.

Dr. Eurich defines self-awareness as the will and skill to understand who we are, including things like our values, patterns, and impact on others. She believes we have internal self-awareness and external self-awareness, which amounts to the difference between how we see ourselves and how others see us. Dr. Eurich's study conducted ten separate investigations with nearly five thousand participants and concluded that only approximately 10 to 15 percent actually fit the criteria for self-awareness.

Like Dr. Eurich's research suggests, many of us could benefit from self-reflection and a deeper dive into our own self-awareness. I believe self-reflection can be done by exploring who we are and our strengths and weaknesses, studying our patterns, evaluating how we show up in life, determining our values, and assessing whether our values align with how we live our lives.

I almost didn't get to participate in this feedback exercise because I considered not attending the second weekend of the emotional intelligence training. Life was going much better since the first weekend training, and I felt very self-aware. I found myself on the phone with my coach from the first weekend of training, questioning whether I should even attend.

She encouraged me to go, sharing, "I'll respect whatever decision you make, but I'd like to see you take yourself on even further because who knows what you may discover in the next four days of training."

Today, I am grateful beyond words that I decided to attend. This is a perfect example of how we all have room to grow even when things are going well. There's a saying, "The moment you think you know everything, you know little." This experience helped me realize that life is a journey, not a destination, and continuing to grow as a person harnesses the power within.

My husband and I at the training center

## REFLECTIVE QUESTIONS

- Identify your top three strengths and circle your top strength (a.k.a., your superpower).
- Are you able to accept and process feedback, or do you find that you dismiss it?
- Do you believe you could benefit from additional self-discovery?

## GROWTH EXERCISE

- Ask three trusted sources to provide you with feedback. Below is a sample message you could send to a trusted source.
  - *I've carefully selected you to provide me with candid feedback to help me grow. I would appreciate it if you would share what you see as my top three strengths and my top three weaknesses. I welcome you to share at least one thing that you see is working in my life and one thing that is not.*

# CHAPTER 11

# SAYING NO CREATES SPACE FOR HELL YES

———

*"The greatest gift you can give yourself is freedom from what others think."*

ABRAHAM HICKS

"No, I am not going to complete the assignment. I've decided to drop out of the program."

I could hardly believe the words that were coming out of my mouth. I had agreed to sign up for a new three-month training that would allow me to use the insights and skills I had learned from the past two trainings. I signed up without my husband because he said it wasn't for him. I admired that he didn't think twice about his decision even though he knew I was disappointed.

I was hesitant to sign up without him because both trainings allowed me to discover that I desired to spend more quality time with my family and less time working.

*Am I doing the opposite of what I set out to do?*

I remained steadfast in my decision to sign up because I experienced the positive impact of the first two trainings. I was curious about what else I could learn and discover about myself. With my growth in mind, I committed.

A week later, I found myself in a kick-off meeting held in the same room as the previous weekend trainings. The facilitator began to explain that we were going to do extraordinary things in the next three months with the support of coaches and teammates.

"Yes, it's going to be weekends and weeknights away from your family," the facilitator said bluntly.

An intuitive gut feeling kicked in.

*Is this really what you want, Lauren?*

Our first task was something called the Wheel of Life. This task consisted of eight sections where we had to rate ourselves from one to ten depending on our satisfaction with that area in our life. We then had to set two SMART goals for each section—goals that were specific, measurable, achievable, realistic, and timely.

Vigorously taking notes, I began to think about my goals. I saw the value of this exercise, but my life was full of goals—goals that I almost always achieved. My new goal was taking things off my to-do list, not adding more shit to it.

So I raised my hand and waited for the facilitator to call on me. "Can 'not giving a fuck' be a measurable goal?" Everyone in the room looked at me with a blank stare while a few people cracked a smile.

The facilitator's head tilted slightly to the right, and he said, "Well, I am not sure how you could quantify that, but I suppose we could explore it."

The facilitator continued with his instructions. "Before you leave tonight, you will download an app to your phone that allows your teammates and coaches to communicate with you. You will be an active participant by sharing your progress and commenting on your teammates' progress."

Within minutes of leaving the kick-off meeting, messages through the app began taking over my phone. Another intuitive feeling kicked in, as something didn't feel right. As I was giving my kids a bath the next day, I found myself trying to wash my daughter's hair while simultaneously responding to teammates' messages.

*You are falling back into old patterns, and it's only been a week since the last training. For the love of God, stop trying to do it all and make everyone happy!*

It took only a day for me to notice that the program was making me extremely anxious. Making this realization was significant progress. Prior to the coaching and trainings, I would have remained on autopilot, oblivious to my feelings. I would push myself until I crashed and burned.

*No more pushing your way through life, Lauren.*

It became apparent that the precious time I desired with my family was being diverted to this program, and it was only day two. I didn't need help achieving more goals. I was the master box-checker! I was now empowered to identify destructive patterns in my life. Guilt began to wash over me, knowing that I wasn't honoring my commitment. I didn't want to let anyone down nor did I want anyone to think less of me. My mind and my heart were at battle. My mind kept trying to talk me into why I should still do the program, running scenarios in my head about what people would say about me, but my heart knew the right answer.

*You must drop out.*

As I dried the water off Maya's little body, I grabbed my phone and called my coach to let her know that I would not finish the assignment and planned to remove myself from the program.

*Why is it so hard for me to say no?*

I thought about the grooming that had been programmed in me to say "yes." For years, I watched the women in my family be there for others, even if that meant at the expense of themselves. Everywhere I turned, I was confronted with society's unrealistic expectation to do it *all* as a woman. I got so good at saying "yes" that I forgot how to use the word "no."

My coach was reluctant to accept my decision to withdraw, offering to help me tailor my goals around my family. I valued her flexibility, but trusted my intuitive gut feeling and my heart's true desire.

With firmness in my voice, I said, "I appreciate your suggestions, but this decision is coming from an empowered place and it is a huge breakthrough for me!"

"I understand," she said, still disappointed. "I will need you to talk to the two team captains and the facilitator to inform them of your decision."

Having to explain my decision during each call felt like a deposition. My guilt skyrocketed as they alluded that I would be letting my other teammates down.

*Why do people make saying "no" so hard? No is a complete sentence!*

The program was committed to individual growth, and I knew the program's intentions were pure. Ironically, my decision was evidence that I had grown leaps and bounds using the skills the program had taught me.

It felt liberating using the word "no" and knowing exactly what I wanted and needed in real time. I continued exercising my mind by saying "no" to anything that crossed my path that didn't align with what I actually wanted. If it wasn't allowing me to be present with my family or creating more harmony and passion in my life, it was a hard "no." Saying "no" began to create space in my life, leading me to what would be a life-changing "yes."

Not long after my new love affair with the word "no," the stars began to align. My boss, who had been exploring options based on my resignation, finally got back to me and shared that his old position at corporate headquarters was open. When I read the job description, it aligned perfectly with my strengths and the work-life harmony I was cultivating. Even though I was nervous because the job was 100 percent remote and required managing people, I reminded myself to trust the process. The job offer was a "HELL YES!"

One month after dropping out of the three-month training program and accepting the new job at corporate, I was asked to sit on a planning committee. Our goal was to create an agenda for the annual compliance and ethics senior leadership meeting. Understanding the value of emotional intelligence, I felt adamant that emotional intelligence was a nonnegotiable agenda item as leaders. The group agreed, and we began brainstorming activities for it. We found ourselves hitting roadblock after roadblock as my efforts to secure a speaker and facilitator continued to be denied.

Passionate about emotional intelligence, I wasn't giving up, so I decided to put my new leadership skills to the test and volunteered to facilitate an exercise that I had once participated in at a training. The exercise not only aligned with our company's mission of "winning as one team," but it also allowed people to experience how they showed up in their own lives.

*Did I just volunteer to speak and lead my colleagues? Why am I not feeling afraid?*

I was in shock. I feared presenting in front of others, but I couldn't deny where my heart was pulling me. Had I allowed myself to remain in the three-month training program, I wouldn't have volunteered to facilitate the exercise because I would have been too stressed and consumed by the program. Withdrawing from the program eventually allowed my passions and purpose to discover me. It served as a perfect reminder that saying "no" actually creates space for the things that are meant for a "HELL YES!"

**REFLECTIVE QUESTIONS**

- Name two times in your life when you said "yes," but actually meant "no."
- Who do you let win when your heart and mind battle?
- Do your goals mirror your desires, or do they mirror what you *should* be doing?

# CHAPTER 12

# LET IT FLOW

---

*"Your brain thinks, but your heart knows."*

JOE DISPENZA

A few weeks after I dropped out of the three-month emotional intelligence leadership training, I finally took Stacie's advice and decided to incorporate yoga into my routine. On Instagram, I came across a girl who was my neighbor growing up. She was offering private one-on-one yoga sessions near my house. My heart felt called to do it, so I scheduled an appointment.

There, I found myself once again sitting across from a spiritual yoga teacher named Jenna about to embark on my second one-on-one yoga experience. I was excited, which was surprising considering how anxious I felt in my first session with Stacie.

We chatted a bit, catching up on our families, and then Jenna asked, "So, what brought you here today?"

"I felt the power of using my breath when I had an anxiety attack at work. I really want to continue growing and deepening the relationship I have with myself. I've heard yoga is a great way to do that."

Jenna agreed and suggested we start in a downward-facing dog position, reminding me to focus on my inhale and exhale.

"Let all of the air out of your body," she said.

She placed her hands at the bottom of my back. I felt a slight pressure. As she stood close to me, I could hear her long inhales and deep exhales. It sounded like she was hissing until every last bit of air had emptied from her body. My breath was shallow and faint.

"You are doing great, Lauren. Keep inhaling, soaking up all of the air, and exhale out of your mouth."

Jenna followed her own instructions, which made me feel comfortable to follow her lead. As my exhales began to get louder and longer, I started to feel a release with each exhale.

Neuroscientists have found that shallow breathing limits the diaphragm's range of motion since it is only activating the sympathetic nervous system. Shallow breathing prevents the lower part of the lungs from receiving its full share of oxygenated air—no wonder I felt so anxious and stressed (*Harvard Health Blog*, 2020).

In the middle of a triangle pose, I asked Jenna, "Should I be breathing in or out?"

Jenna smiled, "There is no right way to do this. Just follow where your breath wants to go and give your body what it needs."

*There you go, Lauren, thinking there is a right way to do something! You just need to listen to your body and give it what it needs. Stop overthinking it!*

I took another deep inhale and then exhaled, noticing where my body and breath wanted me to go. While I was still following her cues, I was moving into my natural flow. This feeling was the exact opposite of how I typically moved throughout each day—with forceful strength, determination, and resistance. By the end of our one-on-one session, I could sense a rhythm as my inhale and exhale flowed deeper and more effortlessly.

Each time I found myself practicing on my mat, it became a fertile training ground to connect my mind, body, and spirit. My practice afforded me the opportunity to listen to what I needed as my body guided me where I was supposed to go next. I began listening to my body off the mat, despite when my mind was telling me to do something else, like push myself to clean the house when I was tired.

My practice on the mat taught me how to further let go of control while I was off the mat—allowing things to come and go much like my inhales and exhales. On the mat, I learned how to get comfortable with being uncomfortable. Just when I thought I couldn't hold a pose any longer, I'd find my breath and be able to settle in more deeply. When I found myself in uncomfortable situations off the mat, I'd revert back to my breath. I could feel the power and peace within me growing as my practice increased both on and off the mat. I became proficient at listening to what felt right in the moment versus what I *should* be doing and taking notice of what was right in front of me while having more compassion for myself and others.

In some classes, I found myself lying in a child's pose while everyone else continued to move around me. It was a simple, but profound gesture that I was allowing myself to do what my body needed despite being instructed to move with the rest of the group. I was allowing my heart to lead while staying conscious of what my mind was thinking in each and every moment.

I asked Jenna why her breath was so loud and intense during our practice.

"As a teacher and guide, I act as a mirror. I hold space for you to feel balanced and express a release," she said.

The simple act of hearing and witnessing Jenna's inhales and exhales created space for me to do the same. Sure, there was a bit of uneasiness. I felt some resistance at first because it was so different and new, but I learned that old patterns don't open new doors.

I was curious why sometimes Jenna recommended breathing out of my mouth while other times I was instructed to breathe out of my nose.

Her answer resonated with me, "When you inhale deeply and release it through your nose, you are calling back your attention and grounding yourself back into your body. This allows you to shift away from the mind and back into your heart space. Breathing out of your mouth allows you to release what is no longer serving you. Yoga and the breath are mechanisms to awaken your life by bringing all of your systems and senses into your own awareness."

I was used to feeling scattered and all over the place. Being in my head blocked me from tapping into my heart's desires and prevented my passions and purpose from discovering me. I had desires and hidden gems that I didn't even know existed because my mind was too busy hijacking my power. My breath, which was always with me, helped to ground me and allowed me to release anything I was holding on to. Even on good days, I found myself setting alarms on my phone as reminders to pause and breathe.

Pausing to fully inhale and exhale became a critical part of my routine because that act of *doing* had become ingrained in every fiber of my being. Meditation and savasana felt uncomfortable because the act of doing nothing made me feel guilty for wasting my precious time. This guilt stemmed from years of conditioning and unconscious psychological protective patterns to keep me safe. The act of doing became my crutch, keeping me so busy that I didn't have time to feel my feelings.

While reflecting off my mat, I realized not feeling my emotions started at a young age. The first time I can recall was when my dad found me organizing our family's pantry the night before his brain surgery—the same surgery he wasn't supposed to wake up from. It was too painful for me to watch the movie with the rest of my family, so I found something else to do.

Despite the discomfort of doing nothing on my mat, I could feel my body craving more of it. Over time, the act of doing nothing grounded me back into my power and renewed my energy. No longer did I find myself daydreaming of being on vacation to get away from the madness. Yoga started to bring me the same feelings of aliveness and peace that I feel on vacations.

Jenna explained, "The power of the yoga practice is that you can find relief without the need to go anywhere. So many of us have been conditioned to believe that we need to escape from our current situation in order to overcome it."

Jenna's words validated a hard lesson that I had learned— specifically, that things outside of myself would not bring me the peace, passion, and sense of purpose I was desperately seeking as I continued to move from job to job.

So many times, I felt like yoga and meditation weren't working and that it was actually preventing me from doing what I actually needed to get done. But my consistent effort allowed me to practice becoming fully conscious of my power. It afforded me sacred time to reacquaint myself and discover parts of myself I didn't know existed. It wasn't always easy, but it dawned on me that is why Stacie initially called it "the practice" and not yoga. *The power is in the practice.* It takes patience to become an observer of your own life and not a victim of your thoughts and behaviors. It takes practice to get out of your own way and step into your natural flow. After all, they say repetition is the mother of all skills.

I wasn't the only one seeing my resistance dissipate and the positive effects of my flow on and off the mat. Several of my friends and colleagues told me that I seemed so different now—so calm and energized.

My workout trainer told me, "I love seeing how happy you are. You never seem stressed anymore. You just go with the flow and seem to be able to do everything you want."

He was right. I had transformed from the inside out by becoming conscious of my blocks, continuously working on them, learning to be comfortable while being uncomfortable, and practicing flowing with life.

I can recall my most sacred flow. The candles flickered their light in the dark room as the frost sat on the windows. Instrumental music played in the background, just slightly louder than Jenna's cues as tears began to stream down my face while my body moved effortlessly through the sequence. I lost myself in the music, and my mind was no longer thinking about what came next; my body just knew how to flow. My tears were not from utter joy, nor were they coming from a place of sadness. They were neutral. My body was releasing what no longer served me while my heart appreciated the fullness of my contentment and ease.

The yoga studio where I experienced my sacred flow

My practice taught me how to dance with life. I became a ballerina, continuously refining my skills, practicing gliding in and out of my thoughts and feelings, and allowing my heart to lead.

**REFLECTIVE QUESTIONS**

- Do you allow yourself to feel/sit with painful and uncomfortable feelings, or do you stuff them?
- Are you so distracted by your thoughts that you cannot feel what your body is trying to tell you?
- Are you willing to practice doing nothing for five minutes without feeling guilty by creating sacred time to just *be*?

**GROWTH EXERCISE**

- Breathing is connected to your life force. Without the breath, you couldn't survive, so take advantage of your breath and explore this breathing exercise to overcome a busy mind (Perrotta, 2020).

  - Step 1: With your eyes opened or closed, take your right thumb and use it to close your right nostril. Inhale through your left nostril for the count of four.

  - Step 2: At the top of your inhale, close your left nostril with your ring finger and lift your thumb to release your right nostril. Out of your right nostril, breathe out slowly for the count of four.

  - Step 3: Keeping your left nostril closed, breathe in through your right nostril for the count of four. Close the right nostril with your right thumb and release your left nostril. Breathe out of your left nostril for the count of four.

  - Step 4: Repeat this process as many times as desired.

# CHAPTER 13

# THE POWER OF YOUR BELIEFS

———

*"The only limits you have are the ones you believe."*

WAYNE DYER

I believed I had no choice but to go to law school. When I told one of my good friends about my plans, she laughed, thinking that I was joking. I also got a confused look from my dad when I shared the news, likely because he was aware of my academic struggles that began in elementary school.

As I was growing up, he'd find himself sitting next to me, helping me read and summarize book reports since it was difficult for me to read. We'd recite spelling words and do flash cards over and over again. As my frustrations grew, so did the late-night hours, which forced my dad to do things for me. This became a pattern, and I unconsciously formed a belief that I couldn't do things by myself because I wasn't smart enough.

It didn't help that my report cards read something like, "A pleasure to have in class, but struggles to understand and apply concepts," or that I failed to read an entire book on my own until high school. Since I believed that everyone went to college, I found myself taking the SAT and ACT. Despite multiple attempts and prep courses, my standardized test scores remained in the bottom 20 percent. My belief that I was not smart enough was further confirmed after I was accepted into the University of Dayton on a conditional basis, where I was expected to participate in the supported instruction (SI) program for the duration of my first year.

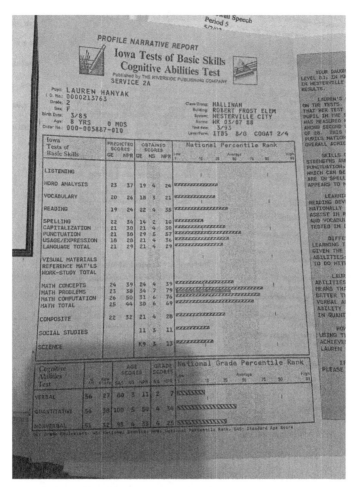

My report card indicating I was below average

My self-discovery process revealed that my struggles with school had formed a core negative belief that I would always need to try harder than others and that I would require assistance if I wanted to make it. Ever since I was a little girl, I remembered my uncle Kenny Bob chanting a little motto, "Just remember to utilize your resources, baby!" His "go get 'em" mentality and positive spin on receiving assistance helped alleviate my feelings that getting help was a bad thing. It's likely why I bartered with my college roommate to do my reports in exchange for folding her clothes and cleaning her room.

Given that I was more like Elle Woods from *Legally Blonde*, with the exception of my brown hair, I can see why people were taken aback when I shared that I was studying for the LSAT. The decision to go to law school was carefully thought out—so I thought. As college graduation approached, everyone said to pick a career. Yet nobody teaches you how to do that, so my subconscious fears began paving the way for me.

My top priority was to pick a career that allowed me to become financially self-sufficient. After my dad's brain tumor, I knew that life could change overnight and I needed to be prepared. I witnessed my mom struggle to support herself and vowed I wouldn't need to depend on anyone for financial support. Being prepared required money, knowledge, and planning. Not to mention, I wanted to give my family the same wonderful experiences my mom and dad afforded me and my siblings.

These experiences contributed to forming another core belief that I must be financially stable and self-sufficient if I wanted to be safe and happy. This belief carried a lot of emotional pain, and it began to trump my belief that I wasn't smart enough to go to law school. While I was interested in becoming a psychiatrist, I was told that it was difficult to get paid by insurance companies. I immediately put blinders on, and law school became the only path to financial security. Clearly, I didn't ask the million-dollar question to enough lawyers regarding their income and debt ratio. I justified that

I'd still be able to help other people practicing law and never once thought about whether it was something I'd actually like to do. After all, *Law & Order* is pretty fucking cool. Like clockwork, history began to repeat itself. My LSAT scores demonstrated I was not law school material and I didn't have a fighting chance to get into any schools, which forced me to take a year off. I kept hearing my uncle's motto in the back of my head, "Utilize your resources, baby!" So that is exactly what I did. I found the best LSAT tutor and closely evaluated what schools could be a possible fit. Low score after low score, never once did they waiver my belief of what was possible for me, though I did find it a bit alarming that practically every attorney told me to run for the hills.

My hard work and belief that I would go to law school paid off because in the summer of 2004, I was conditionally accepted to the Ohio Northern University Pettit College of Law, where I was required to take two first-year classes over the summer to see if I could "make it" before the rest of the first-year class arrived in the fall. I found myself reading things twice to fully comprehend them, using the extra support the school provided, and creating study groups with students who were also accepted on a conditional basis.

I consistently put in the work and found myself passing classes. In an effort to maximize my time, I took my notes to the gym and read over them as I ran on the treadmill. I found myself visualizing walking across the stage and being handed my diploma instead of reading my notes that I was supposed to be studying. I didn't realize what I was doing at the time, but the power of visualization allowed me to create resonance in my body of what it would feel like to graduate from law school. Each time I found myself doing it, I had chills running throughout my body. These clear visualizations of my end goal, coupled with my belief that I could do it, no doubt led to my successful graduation in three years, just like the other students, despite the statistical odds stacked against me. My law school experience demonstrated the power of belief! After graduating from law school, my core belief was perpetuated, showing me again that I can only be successful if I worked harder than everyone else. I convinced myself that I was admitted into the bar by mistake and that I just got lucky. I couldn't let people find out that I was a fraud, so I found myself setting unrealistic expectations and embodying perfectionistic qualities—qualities like having a fear of failing, procrastinating, being highly critical, having an all-or-nothing mentality, being driven by fear, results focused, feeling depressed by unmet goals, and becoming wired to be hypercritical of small mistakes. These core beliefs unconsciously dictated my actions.

Being continuously asked to think about what I was pretending not to know about myself at the emotional intelligence leadership training and taking notice of my negative thought patterns and false beliefs highlighted my perfectionistic qualities. My mind constantly debated whether or not I was a perfectionist because there were sides of me outside of work where I was free-spirited, decisive, confident, and funny. The debate went on for years until I received spontaneous clarity while hugging my coach goodbye at the emotional intelligence training.

I realized I was a perfectionist only in the areas I believed I was not good enough. It suddenly made sense why I took certain actions in some areas of my life and not others. It was the first time that I realized this unconscious belief of not being good enough was causing me to work myself to death. These actions led to being anxious, exhausted, and unfulfilled. Once I addressed this belief through daily affirmations, intentionally looking for my daily wins, and setting realistic expectations, I was able to free myself from my own captivity.

Law school showed me that I could do the unthinkable when I believed. I know that when I change my beliefs, I can change my life.

## REFLECTIVE QUESTIONS

- In what areas in your life do you not feel good enough?
- What beliefs, stories, or thoughts do you find repeatedly replaying through your mind?
- Identify what motive, leverage, or emotional pain you can create that will trump your negative beliefs and allow you to take action.
  - Example: I created a belief that if I didn't go to law school, I wouldn't be financially secure, which created leverage that trumped my belief that I wasn't smart enough.
  - Example: I created a belief that if I didn't move my body, I would not have natural energy to carry me through my day, which trumped my belief that I didn't have time to do it.

# CHAPTER 14

# HUMOR HEALS

———

*"Laughter is the greatest weapon we have and we, as humans, use it the least."*

As I sat at my desk firing away emails, I saw a man wearing tan leather shoes strapped with blue shoelaces approach my desk, accompanied by my colleague. The man, who I'd never seen before, had on slim-fitting blue jeans and a tan leather belt paired with a flamboyantly bright-colored button-down shirt. His light brown hair was slightly gelled and perfectly paired with his matching briefcase that hung over his shoulder.

My colleague stood over my desk, smiled, and said, "Hey Lauren, this is John. He is our new compliance officer based out of our Atlanta office. You two will be working a lot together, so I wanted to make the official introduction."

The man held out his hand. "Well, nice to meet you, Lauren. That sure was a fucking whirlwind of a trip to get here. Bless your heart; I don't know how y'all do it. It's cold as hell here!"

I laughed under my breath. It had been a hot minute since I had heard a cuss word at work.

He stopped at the framed wedding picture behind my desk. "Beautiful picture, and the feathers in your hair, just lovely, child. Welp, I better go make myself useful."

I couldn't help but smile ear to ear as he walked away.

*He likes feathers and cusses even more than I do!*

I had no idea who I had just met, but I knew I needed more of him in my life.

Turns out, he was in my next meeting. He looked up as I walked into the conference room.

"Well, well, look who decided to grace us with her presence!"

*Was he talking to me?*

I couldn't help but crack a smile. I didn't expect a comment like that. It was totally outside of the box. Everyone settled into their seats, and the project manager began explaining their new idea. It was a service that would help many patients, but unfortunately, it needed major tweaks by legal and compliance before we could even think about taking it to market.

Without missing a beat, John interjected, "Lord have mercy! Your proposal will require several changes unless y'all like orange jumpsuits or something?"

I almost spat out my coffee and laughed out loud in front of everyone. It was like he read my inner thoughts—the ones I'd never say out loud because I was all about the politically correct and conservative approach at work.

Everyone in the room began laughing at John's comment. It didn't take long before we were exploring other ways to provide the service. It was the first time I had seen someone take this kind of lighthearted and honest approach. It was a breath of fresh air!

Meanwhile, I was drowning in emails. I couldn't seem to make any headway because I was in meetings all day. Many of the emails were complex and required large blocks of time to appropriately respond. Mark, my manager, knew I was overwhelmed because I shared that work was becoming too much, which is why he decided to help me review a few submitted requests.

On our fourth or fifth request, Mark looked up at me and asked, "So what do you think we should do with this one?"

I started to list all of the things I needed to do to answer the request. "Oh, and read the regulation again too."

Mark asked me to keep the request moving. He pushed again. "What do you already know that you can share with them right now?"

"I don't know. I feel like I need more time to evaluate it."

"Lauren," he said, smiling, "I know you want to get this right and you take your work seriously, but you have enough knowledge to take action right now without having to read anything."

*Damn straight I take my work seriously. I am not about to put my name on something I don't feel 110 percent confident in.*

"Think of your mind as a muscle," he said. "Each time you take immediate action, you are strengthening this muscle. Over time, you will get better at using what you know to make faster progress."

*Interesting. This sounds like the book I am listening to by Lisa Nichols.*

We finished a few more requests. I felt like I could breathe again. As I drove home from work, my thoughts felt like they were in a champion ping-pong match. I couldn't get what Mark said out of my mind.

*Did I really take my work too seriously? Was I struggling to get my work done because I'm risk averse, precise, and over-analyze the shit out of everything?*

*Lauren, you know there is always a "right" answer, and it's your job to provide it.*

*But sometimes the law is gray. Maybe there isn't a "right" answer and you just tell them what you know.*

*What the hell is a "right" answer anyway?*

*Should I stop being so serious and start taking more messy action by just telling the business what I already know?*

*When did I become all serious anyway?*

I remember when I was a little girl, I was always demonstrating my latest gymnastics and dance moves for anyone who would watch me, making crafts and bracelets for friends and family, cooking and laughing with my grandmother, and playing school where I was always the teacher.

Slowly but surely, I lost my childlike qualities. I couldn't identify one particular event but realized it was small gradual shifts over time. So small that I didn't notice—from gymnastics and diving meets that required precise movements for high scores to losing confidence in my ability to do academic work on my own. I shot fake MTV videos with friends, insisting that I be the backup dancer because it was too risky to be the leader.

In college, years after my dad's brain tumor, I assumed responsibility for his finances and health care, causing me to live in fear that I would mess things up beyond the complex state in which I inherited them. Everything had to be done right. I had to have all of the details, analyze all avenues, and validate every decision with experts to prevent future hardship.

Mark's comment allowed me to reflect. It deepened my consciousness around my strict way of being. I couldn't help but find it ironic that the Universe had strategically placed John in my life the week that Mark shared these insights with me.

The second John saw me getting flustered or in my head, I'd get a "child, don't get your panties in a bunch over there." His constant reminders snapped me back into reality, which slowly began to retrain my mind for the present moment. He'd kindly remind me that we weren't performing brain surgery and that things didn't have to be perfect.

Later that week, John and I found ourselves sitting alone in a private conference room on a call. We were on mute and the presenter was on speaker.

As we listened, John blurted out, "Are these fuckers serious?"

He always said exactly what I was thinking. His humor wasn't limited to his comments. We'd find ourselves in meetings with other people, and he would send me a text of funny memes if he saw me taking things too seriously. The memes ranged from a picture of a dumpster on fire rolling down a hill with a customized caption like "Shit's on fire, don't touch it" to a simple smiley face. John's presence and humor turned what had become tense, long, and stressful weeks into something less dreadful.

I found myself taking Mark's advice and began taking more immediate action, though I still sometimes needed validation. I'd present John with facts and my analysis for his insight.

"Sounds good to me. Go with God, honey! Your guess is as good as mine."

Questions that were extra complex would be followed with, "Yes ma'am! I ain't got no more fucks to give."

His humor and childlike behavior helped me take a more lighthearted approach, which significantly reduced my stress and anxiety. I later learned that clinical studies and research suggest that humor and laughter can improve not only clinical outcomes, like cancer and heart disease, but can also reduce physiological responses like stress or anxiety and improve your mood, self-esteem, and coping mechanisms (MacDonald, 2004). There was no doubt I was benefitting from John's humor, as I was constantly smiling when I was around him.

Friday arrived, and I was shocked by how quickly the week had gone. Weeks without John felt like eternities. I was relieved to hear that he would be spending much of his time in the Columbus office with me. As I was relaxing in bed that Friday evening, a text displayed on my phone from John.

"This old bitch has landed over yonder."

His text was followed by a handful of ridiculous memes, humorous videos, and senseless pictures depicting our stressful week. As his texts continued to roll in, so did my belly laughs, which turned into tears.

"Who are you talking to?" my husband asked.

"This guy named John. I just started working with him this week. You'll need to meet him. He is so funny!"

John's humor provided such a release and lightened my load. It made me realize I hadn't laughed in such a long time and reminded me that I took life too seriously. I saw firsthand how people are placed in our lives for a reason. They can help us grow, if we allow it. John and Mark not only disrupted my normal, but they demonstrated it's okay to take action even if you don't feel like you have all of the information.

More importantly, you can have fun while doing hard things! Lightheartedness and humor are choices that can be brought to any situation if we choose them.

**REFLECTIVE QUESTIONS**

- Name one thing you can do to incorporate more humor or lightheartedness into your life.
- What is one step you could do today to exercise your "take action" muscle?
- Do you believe there is a correct answer for everything?

# CHAPTER 15

# UNICORNS

---

*"The beauty you see in me is a reflection of you."*

RUMI

I began to notice a pattern in my life. No matter what job I had, I was comparing myself to other women around me who just seemed to have it all together—the special unicorns. It never failed. As I jumped from job to job, I would always discover at least one. A unicorn is confident, smart, witty, quick on their feet, compassionate, but most importantly, appears calm and at peace. Very little would ruffle a unicorn's feathers.

I remember meeting my first unicorn. It was Wednesday and I wished it were Friday. I sat in my office, with no natural light in sight, as I waited on the phone for a female partner at a prestigious law firm to join. I had not worked with her, but needed her expertise, which left me feeling insecure. She joined the line, and I was greeted by a smooth, steady, and alert voice.

In complete hustle mode, I said, "Hi, I am Lauren. Thanks so much for jumping on this call. I am concerned because the business probably wants to violate research regulations and . . ."

She interrupted me. "Hi! I believe this is the first time we've met. Should we take a minute to introduce ourselves?" My shoulders sank, and I looked down at the floor as I let out a sigh.

*Seriously, Lauren, you can't even take a minute to allow for introductions. For God's sake, all you're worried about is jumping into business.*

It was not infrequent that something like this would happen, where I would be moving so fast that I would forget the importance of simple formalities like introductions, eye contact, or a simple "how are you doing?" Her interruption allowed me to take a breath and introduce myself. She went on to clearly articulate the problem and solution. During the conversation, my mind was racing, working hard to comprehend all of the information, as I tried to stay a few steps ahead to think of what questions I had. My mind was constantly moving at the speed of a rocket ship headed for space, except what I was doing wasn't as mind-blowing as NASA.

As I hung up the phone, I sat back in my chair and collapsed. Staring at the white wall in front of me, I felt trapped in a small cage, wondering why I couldn't be more like her.

*Why can't I communicate complex information in such a flawless and digestible manner with confidence and ease?*

"Why can't I be more like her?" was a regular thing when it came to special unicorns. These unicorns were not limited to women at work. I found myself admiring others outside of work like my dad, uncle, and my roommate's dad, who all had wild ideas that they turned into businesses. I realized these unicorns had commonalities. Many were creative entrepreneurs, intelligent in their own ways, and each had unwavering confidence and humility in themselves. Because I was so busy, constantly stressed, and anxious, it took years to make the connection that what I was noticing in these unicorns actually lived deep within myself.

After ten years of practicing law, I met the most radiant unicorn of them all, Faith. She was a chief privacy officer for a Fortune 10 company. I was about to interview with her and found myself sitting in a large, empty conference room. A phone sitting on top of a large oval conference table was on speaker. I anxiously waited for Faith to join the line as I swiveled back and forth in my chair. She joined the call, and I was greeted by a warm, rich, and calming voice.

"Hi, Lauren, it's Faith! How are you today? Such a pleasure speaking with you!" she exclaimed. "I am very impressed by your résumé and experience. Do you have a preference for the compliance side or legal side?"

*Do I even like either?*

"I prefer the compliance side. I find that I have an opportunity to improve things, whereas on the legal side, I am just reacting to fire drills."

Faith went on to ask me questions about an investigation I worked on with the Office for Civil Rights.

*Holy shit, she even read my résumé.*

Her question took me by surprise because the person who had interviewed me prior to Faith didn't read my résumé. That interview felt rushed, forced, and impersonal. As I got off the phone with Faith, I began to admire the beautiful view of the city, feeling so special and seen. The thought of working in Faith's organization with other privacy professionals had me grinning ear to ear. It was the first time that I had the opportunity to work alongside a team of experts led by an intelligent and experienced leader like Faith. I was elated when I got the job.

At first, my contact with Faith was minimal. But as the business issues increased in complexity and risk, I found myself on more calls with her. She was always grounded and peaceful. Nothing seemed to rattle her, and she never seemed to be rushed despite the fact that she was in back-to-back meetings all day long. She always gave her undivided attention. I constantly wanted to make a good impression, so I found myself rehearsing what I'd say to her and obsessively rereading anything I'd write. Overcompensating was my standard to ensure she wouldn't find out I wasn't always sure of what I was doing.

I found myself in a tense situation where the business didn't like the advice I had given them, so they decided to climb the corporate ladder to get the opinion they "wanted" from Faith. Constantly being pushed around by the business sucked the life out of me, leaving me feeling as though I had been strangled. It was a defeating cycle that affected the energy I could offer to my family and exacerbated my thoughts of "I am not enough."

I was intimately familiar with the legal issues, yet there I found myself on a plane headed to Atlanta to defend my position. A *People* magazine sat in the seat pocket in front of me. I wanted to read it so badly, but I couldn't allow myself. I continued to study my notes and past emails to ensure I was prepared. The plane landed and I placed my papers into a manila folder. For whatever reason, printed paper gave me a sense of security. As I slid the folder into my bag, the *People* magazine caught my eye one last time.

*Next time, you can read it.*

We found ourselves in a large conference room waiting for the unicorn herself to arrive. She sat down at the head of the table with her notebook and pen next to her. She wrapped her shawl around her shoulders, waiting for someone to start the meeting. The business members who doubted my advice presented for at least ten minutes before Faith interrupted with a shocking statement.

"I need you to back up and give me the dummy version."

My head shot up.

*Did she just say she needed the dummy version? Holy shit! This is the oracle herself!*

She had just vocalized my worst fear. I felt like I constantly needed the dummy version, as I was constantly pushing myself to overcompensate for my inadequacies. I couldn't understand how these words just flowed effortlessly out of her mouth with such ease and authority. She sat patiently, self-assured, waiting for the business to provide her with more details.

Right then and there, I had a breakthrough. I just needed to practice being fully honest with myself in what I knew. I needed to stop judging myself so harshly when I didn't know something or when I wasn't grasping it easily. I was enough, and there was no need to overcompensate.

I continued to watch and study Faith's way of being since I wanted to embody more of her traits. During a Tony Robbins's training that I attended, he called this "modeling." It is when you find someone who is steps ahead of where you want to be and you observe them and mimic their behaviors and actions. Robbins believes that modeling will save you heartache and time because that person is able to teach you what they know, saving you time and energy.

Not long after the meeting, I asked Faith what influenced her calm and grounded leadership style. I wanted to know whether it was innate or learned.

"I think it is a little bit of both," she said. "Growing up, my parents were calm people who valued continuous education. Being around them certainly rubbed off on me, and I always watch other leaders to see what works and what doesn't. Early on in my career, I was confronted with a difficult situation where I couldn't change the person or what was happening. I listened to a sermon that helped me realize that when I can't change my situation, I can change my perspective and focus on what I am grateful for. I know people aren't going to remember the advice I gave them, but they will remember how I treated them."

Faith's comment affirmed my belief that a person's perspective is incredibly important. I doubt that I am the only person who has identified special unicorns in their life. It is easy for the mind to see wonderful qualities in other people, especially unicorns, which can trigger the mind's inner critic to rage.

*If only I could be as peaceful and calm as her.*
*If only I could have their confidence.*
*If only I could find time to do that with my kids.*
*If only I had the free time that they have, I could be happier.*
*If only I could be as fun and outgoing.*
*If only I had her high-vibe energy.*
*If only I could be that creative.*
*If only I could have her body.*
*If only I could be that smart.*
*If only I had their job.*
*If only I could have their discipline, I could make things happen too.*

*If only I could make decisions like them, maybe I could make progress.*

*If only I could make the money they do, I could finally do what I wanted.*

*If only.*

*If only.*

*If only.*

The mind's perspective is powerful. I realized that what I was constantly seeing in others actually lived inside me, but it was buried underneath limiting beliefs. Through my sacred morning time and yoga practice, I began to cultivate the steadfast confidence and peace that I saw in other unicorn leaders. My marvel for creative entrepreneurs led me to understand that I wanted to create my own business. Prior to my self-discovery journey, my mind wouldn't allow me to fathom the idea. I was able to discover it by learning about myself and believing that these hidden gems were waiting for me to uncover them.

**REFLECTION QUESTIONS:**
- What qualities do you constantly see in others that you wish you had or embodied?
- What beliefs do you need to shift in order to embody what you see in your unicorns?
- What actions do you need to take to embody the qualities of your unicorns?

**GROWTH EXERCISE**
- Make a list of your special unicorns. These individuals are people you admire who can be living or dead. They could be a neighbor or a celebrity that you've never met. When you create a list of people, think about the qualities

you love about them. Is it a personality trait, the way they look, the way they treat other people, or their occupation? Use this list as a clue to identify what actually lives within you, even if you can't see it on the surface.

# CHAPTER 16

# DIVINE IMPRINTS

———

*"Life will give you whatever experience is most helpful for the evolution of your consciousness."*

ECKERT TOLLE

In 2017, I gave birth to the biggest surprise of my life, a baby girl. I was in the beginning stages of my inward quest when my mother-in-law said, "Isn't it beautiful how these little creatures of love are so innocent and pure blank slates that you get to mold?"

*Huh? A blank slate?*

As a psychology undergrad, I had studied nature versus nurture—nature being biological traits and other attributes you are born with and nurture where you are shaped by your environment, upbringing, life experiences, and societal conditioning. I refer to these as divine imprints. I've never found that one trumped the other, though I did see how both impacted my thoughts, actions, and how I showed up in my own life. I had always been fascinated that my sister, brother, and I were so different, yet we were all raised by the same loving parents in the same environment and had similar experiences. At times, it certainly seemed as if nature was the predominant factor.

When I'd talk to my mom about how my life experiences have shaped me, she was quick to point out that many qualities, such as my need for control, were apparent at a very young age. As a baby, I made someone hold my bottle even if I could hold it myself. In order for me to go to sleep at night, someone had to rock me until I was sound asleep. I'd refuse to wear bows at the age of three, not because they were uncomfortable, but to demonstrate that I was in control. My mom shared that I'd go around the home and meticulously place hangers outside of all of our doors. Each hanger had its exact place and needed to go in a certain order. As I got older, I wouldn't allow my mom to do my laundry or pack my lunches because she couldn't do it right. My need for control was then perpetuated by nurture related factors, my dad's brain tumor being the most significant.

Life, as I knew it, was normal one day and then the next it wasn't. It was a hot summer day, and I was eating my breakfast and watching TV when I heard a knock at the front door. It was my mom's best friend, Julie. They had just left the house to go walking.

"Hey honey, I need you to get your brother and sister. You guys are going to come to my house for a bit. Your mom has to go give your dad something."

As I stood in my closet deciding what shirt to put on, I could sense something was wrong. My eyes started to fill up with tears as I began to think that something bad had happened to my dad, though the feeling didn't last more than a few seconds. I finished getting ready and met Julie downstairs so we could walk to her house.

As I sat in Julie's living room watching TV, I happened to look out her window to see my dad's car. It appeared that my dad had ran his car into a tree, which happened to be five short feet from a large pond.

"Julie, is that my dad's car?"

"No honey, I don't think so."

"Julie, I know that's my dad's car. What happened?"

"Your dad got in an accident and he's at the hospital. Your mom is there with him now. She should be calling shortly."

An MRI showed that my dad had a brain tumor in his frontal lobe that was larger than a baseball. Though I didn't know it at the time, he wasn't supposed to live through surgery. He was allowed to come home the night before his surgery, which was a few days after his accident. My family decided to watch a movie, but I couldn't seem to pay attention to it or sit still. Instead, my dad found me in our pantry obsessively organizing and cleaning it, perfectly placing each can just so.

That was one of my first memories of my incessant inability to sit with my feelings and yet another example of seeking control. This life experience, coupled with the changes that came after my dad's surgery, changed the trajectory of my life. It became an event that unconsciously shaped my thoughts and actions. My parents bent over backward trying to make things normal, but my childhood was never the same again. I learned how to be "normal" even when things were not normal. As an observant and responsible older sibling, I found myself as the "go-to" person to fix things when trouble arose.

Over time, I saw that I didn't come into this world as a blank slate. Rather, I had distinguishable imprints at birth and gathered more imprints along the way based on my life experiences. These divine imprints helped form my mindset and shape my consciousness. I found that information and events were always being funneled through my divine imprints, affecting how I interpreted and digested information. For example, I interpreted a piece of information, such as my dad's brain tumor, that bad things were going to happen and I needed to plan and be prepared. On the other hand, the event made my sister realize that life is precious and she should go travel the world because who knows what tomorrow will bring.

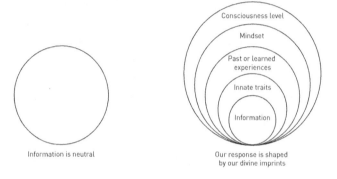

Information is neutral

Our response is shaped by our divine imprints

While I would consider my dad's brain tumor a traumatic event, I've found that nontraumatic events can equally impact a person's divine imprints. For example, my friends and family laughing at me when I told them I was going to law school left a significant imprint that I now realize diverted me away from my authentic self; I was too laser focused on proving that I could.

I believe that I came into this world with certain traits and was meant to have certain experiences that would help evolve my consciousness. Understanding my divine imprints helped me become clear of where my beliefs and interpretations originated. They also helped me see the root cause of negative beliefs that affected my mindset and hijacked my innate power.

When obstacles are placed in my path, I now see them as lessons and growing opportunities to further expand my consciousness. I now find that continual tests help guide me back to my highest self and are not placed in my path to make my life hell. I used to think that life was happening to me, but I now realize it is happening for me!

When I find myself in rough patches, I've turned to astrology, having hired professionals to look at my charts and give me guidance. Marga Laube, the author of *Agents of Evolution*, compares astrology to a weather forecast.

"A meteorologist can provide you with insights and guidance. You check the weather from time to time because you want to know how to prepare in case the forecast calls for rain. Of course, the meteorologist may not always be 100 percent accurate, but the forecast provides you with helpful insights. The same is true about astrology. It can help prepare you for what season is ahead, allowing you to use your energy appropriately and pace yourself, knowing this too shall pass. The beauty of astrology is that while something may be forecasted, we always have access to free will."

Marga shared, "I once had a client who loved growing food in her garden. She worked for an insurance company and had a family, but wasn't fully fulfilled. Her astrological charts demonstrated her love for food and people were not being fully expressed, so she decided to open up a bed and breakfast. A year later, I followed back up with her, and she shared how fulfilled and grateful she was that her astrological charts could provide her with such insights to make that shift."

Much like a puzzle, I pieced together my divine imprints to form a holistic picture of why I do things the way I do. My life no longer felt cloudy because I had a clear understanding to work from. When things would pop up, like a stressful situation at work, I would find myself able to immediately notice my emotions and behavior, allowing me to consciously direct how I wanted to handle the situation or how much energy I wanted to exert.

My inward reflections demonstrated that these divine imprints shaped how I showed up in my life, whether I was conscious of them or not. Each time I become an observer of my own life, I reclaim my power through my consciousness as I funnel facts and events through my divine imprints that affect my experience.

**REFLECTIVE QUESTIONS**
- Identify three innate traits that you believe you were born with (Nature).
- Name three life events, childhood experiences, or environmental factors that have shaped you (Nurture).
- Name one thing or theme that continues to show up in your life over and over again. Do you believe it is a test that continues to be placed in your path so you'll learn a specific lesson?

## CHAPTER 17

# MAKE TIME YOUR BITCH

———

*"The past has no power over us. It doesn't matter how long we have had a negative pattern. The point of power is in the present moment. What a wonderful thing to realize! We can begin to be free in this moment!"*

LOUISE HAY

Time was a big struggle for me, but I learned how to make it my bitch. This helped change my beliefs around time and how I manage it. Time is our most valuable resource. I found myself complaining that I never had enough time since I was constantly catering to everybody else's needs. I was convinced that if I had more time, I would be less stressed and would have the time to do what I needed and wanted to do, which would make me feel happier.

The little free time I did have, I'd spend it on unproductive and destructive things like complaining, binge drinking to relieve stress, or feeding my fears. One specific drinking incident demonstrated that life was running me versus me running it. The incident woke me up and made me reevaluate how I was using my time.

My 'Sunday scaries' were out of control, and instead of preparing lunches for the week, I found myself drinking with neighbors as our kids played outside. Let's just say a bottle of champagne was my appetizer, and we were now well on our way to dessert. Drinking always took the edge off and masked my stress and anxiety. It didn't take long for the drinks to suppress my 'Sunday scaries.' Carefree Lauren was out to play. The music was pumping and I was drunk, dancing on our backyard dining table, raising the roof and twerking without a care in the world.

Monday morning hit me like a ton of bricks. I woke up in a panic, trying to piece together the night because I had blacked out.

*Lauren! What is going on! Yes, Brian told you that you bathed the kids and helped put them to bed, but you gotta get your shit together!*

I felt ashamed and concerned that my drinking was taking me to new, dark territories. As I was getting the kids ready for school the next morning, a song came on and Brody shouted, "Mom!" I looked over and my one-year-old daughter was raising the roof and twerking her little butt up and down.

"Mom! Maya is doing that happy dance you were doing on the table yesterday," Brody exclaimed.

I gasped for air. It was a blunt reality check that my kids were watching exactly how I was spending my time. I couldn't bear the thought of my kids only seeing me in a fun and carefree state when I was drinking. I wanted to understand how I was using my time. I knew the value of tracking my energy and patterns because it helped me prepare for a big meeting with my boss, so I decided to write down where I spent my time and how I felt about it.

I took one of my journals and drew a line down the middle of it. On the left-hand side, I wrote down everything I spent time on that stressed me out, caused anxiety, was boring, or things that I spent time on out of fear of upsetting someone or to prevent something bad from happening. On the right-hand side, I listed everything that I desired, enjoyed doing, felt peaceful and content while doing it, or felt excited about.

It didn't take long to realize that I was giving my time and power away to things that did not excite me or stressed me out. While I absolutely love Costco, the Sunday adventure became mundane. I recall driving home one Sunday thinking, "This can't be the rest of my life." I found myself spending time on things that fed my fears, like dedicating an absurd amount of time to work so others wouldn't figure out that I was a fraud.

I felt sad that very little of what I spent my time on made it to the right-hand side of my list. I constantly thought about volunteering, but there was never any time. I began to think about Albert Einstein's definition of insanity, "Doing the same thing over and over again and expecting a different result." If I continued to use my time for things that were the complete opposite of what I wanted, then how could I justify my time here on Earth? I knew if it was meant to be, it was up to me.

*What do you want, Lauren?*

I desired not to be so rushed. I wanted to read books, have more fun with my kids, spend more time outside, and help organizations that I felt passionate about. I wanted to work on meaningful things, obtain a privacy certification, fix our back deck, rent a boat, and do yoga several times a week. My initial desires were very risk averse. My mind was still in training to think in a limitless manner, so it was operating rationally and analytically.

I continued to exercise my mind to think outside of the box. It didn't take long before I had more items on my desired list—things like taking spontaneous trips, buying a boat, learning how to pole dance, traveling to Italy and Greece, going on spiritual retreats, traveling around the world with my kids, sleeping outside in a hut built into a tree, owning my own business that helped other people, taking family and friends on an all-inclusive paid vacation, and building a custom home on the water.

With my desires clarified, I began to think about what I truly valued. I did a brain dump and wrote down any values that came to mind.

# LIST OF VALUES

acceptance
adventure
cheerfulness
compassion
confidence
contribution
courage
creativity
decisiveness
dedication
determination
empathy
equality
excellence
family
flexibility
freedom
going with the flow
grit
happiness
harmony
having fun
health & vitality
honesty

humor
individuality
influence
inner peace
integrity
intimacy
learning & continued growth
lighthearted
love
making an impact
money & abundance
nature
passion
relationships
respect
responsibility
security
simplicity
spirituality
stability
strategy
success
taking risks
teamwork & community
trust

I knew my top value was inner peace. I vowed that anything I spent my time on would be in line with that value. While I didn't love all aspects of my job, it brought me inner peace knowing my family was financially supported. Plus, after working through my imposter syndrome, I felt more confident and at peace while at work. Since I experience joy when having fun with my family, I hired a cleaning lady and stopped living in fear that we would need the money. Instead of cleaning, I would take my kids to the pool, which made my heart happy.

I hated to see that I was feeding my fears and not doing things that I truly valued with my time. I realized that my inability to be clear about what I wanted, coupled with actions rooted in fear, prevented me from moving forward with my actual desires. It was a vicious cycle.

I took a red pen to my time audit notes and crossed out anything I no longer wanted to spend time on. My red pen was busy. Working late at night and on weekends—out. Cleaning my house—out. Cooking dinner every night—out. With a blue pen, I then added items to my desires list like reading, date night during the week with my kids, renting a boat, shutting my work computer off by 6:00 p.m., more yoga and meditation, and removing my work email from my personal phone. As I incorporated more desires into my life that aligned with my values, I noticed my energy, positive vibrations, and fulfillment increasing.

Two months after I dropped out of the three-month emotional intelligence leadership training, the New Year rolled around and I completed the Wheel of Life. The Wheel of Life had eight categories: Money/Abundance, Fun/Creativity, Health/Well-being, Love Life, Family/Friends, Spirituality, Self-Care/Personal Growth, and Career/Passion. I rated myself from one to ten in each area. One represented not very satisfied and ten represented very satisfied. These ratings helped me assess where I wanted to focus my time.

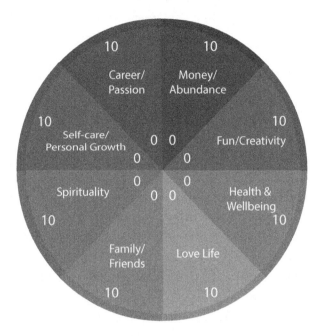

WHEEL OF LIFE
0 Unsatisfied
10 Extremely Satisfied

Rank each category and write
one goal for each category

My scores showed that my lowest areas were Fun/Creativity, Love Life, and Career/Passion. I set one goal for each area and backed each goal with sub-goals. I focused my time on my lowest three categories. My Love Life goal was to learn how to salsa dance with my husband. My sub-goals included researching dance studios and private trainers in town, selecting a studio or trainer, and committing to a time and regular cadence. We agreed upon a one-hour lesson every other week.

Each day, I found myself creating a list of three things that would be completed by the end of the day. This was a steep departure from operating off my never-ending to-do list. Setting three tasks each day allowed me to feel accomplished. It not only provided intention for each day, but it also gave me the motivation to tackle the next day, leaving me feeling energized rather than depleted.

For bigger items, like a project that couldn't be completed in one day, I would block off a period of time. My meditation and yoga practice helped me become cognizant that I had the most energy in the morning. I capitalized on that energy by tackling the most challenging items first. On days when I found myself being overly critical or negative, I would spend more time focusing on what I was grateful for.

Law school taught me that if I was very clear on my end goal and mirrored my actions to my desired outcome, anything was possible. Of course, this time, I really focused on *why* I was doing something to ensure it aligned with my true values and not my fears. This new process felt so unnatural. Most of my life, I did what I thought I was supposed to do or *should* do. I was no longer reacting. I was proactively designing a life I loved.

Each and every day, I was raising my vibrational state and taking my power back. I taught people and the Universe how I wanted to be treated by remaining aligned with my values and steadfast to my goals.

**REFLECTIVE QUESTIONS**

- List your top five values.
- Name three things you can delegate that will allow you to spend more time doing things you enjoy and align with your values.
- Do you spend your time doing things in an effort to make other people happy or to prevent something bad from happening?

**GROWTH EXERCISES:**

- Audit how you spend your time. Take a piece of paper and draw a line down the middle of the page. On the left-hand side, list anything that drains you, and on the right-hand side, list what brings you excitement, joy, and peace. Take several days to complete this list.
- Go to mindmusclemotivator.com to complete the Wheel of Life. Bonus points if you do it with an accountability partner.

# CHAPTER 18

# BREADCRUMBS

---

*"Passion is energy. Feel the power that comes from focusing on what excites you!"*

OPRAH WINFREY

Never in my life has anyone told me to pay attention to what brings me energy, what excites me, or what uses my strengths. My parents never forced me to do anything, nor did they steer me one way or the other. It was just ingrained in me to go to school, do well, and get a good job. I was never taught how to go about that process, so I did the best I could with the knowledge and consciousness I had at that time.

After law school, I pondered on the question of what I was supposed to do with my life. I could feel that I had a purpose, but I couldn't articulate it. I got lost and the passion for my life diminished. Yet when I look back, I see that breadcrumbs were left for me, but I wasn't paying attention. If I had followed the breadcrumbs, I probably would have saved myself years of agony. I define breadcrumbs as anything that fascinates you, brings you life and energy, and leaves you curious and excited. Breadcrumbs may seem random, and they may not make sense by themselves. If you are experiencing a breadcrumb, it is likely you will lose track of time.

The first time I took a personality test— the Clifton StrengthsFinder—I was mesmerized. It was my first corporate job. I walked into my colleague's office and noticed a small, framed plastic plaque sitting on her desk that had five bold words beneath it.

"What is this?" I asked.

"Oh, those are my top five strengths. The company pays for us to take a multiple-choice questionnaire that determines your top strengths."

I left her office dying with anticipation to know what mine would be. I knew that I was hardworking and good with people, but I had never stopped to think about my strengths, let alone whether I was using any of them on a day-to-day basis. The questionnaire was straightforward and when my results came back, I found myself studying each word. My report showed that out of thirty-four strengths, my top five were Discipline, Woo, Responsibility, Relator, and Harmony.

My five strengths

*What the hell is a Woo and a Relator?*

I dissected the report to find that Woo stood for winning others over. According to the report, a Woo loves to meet new people and is energized by learning about strangers, whereas the Relator enjoys close relationships with others, finding deep satisfaction in working with friends to achieve a goal.

I found myself reading not only about my strengths in detail, but also about all of the others until I heard a knock on my office door. I looked at the clock, realizing that I had just spent over an hour absorbing its juicy contents. The knock forced me to stop, and I placed the report in my desk drawer. Due to the demands at work, I didn't find myself looking at the report again until two years later.

Looking back, I can say with 100 percent certainty that the Clifton StrengthsFinder assessment was a breadcrumb. I didn't know it at the time because I was so caught up feeding the fears and being overwhelmed that I wasn't able to understand that I should have explored personality tests further because they excited me! Instead, I dismissed it and jumped right back on my automatic hamster wheel.

Around the same time, I had a similar experience when my mom calculated my Numerology Life Path Number. Similar to astrology, it provides you with insights about yourself and your life, such as traits and natural tendencies, obstacles you may face, strengths, weaknesses, and ambitions. As I sat at my mom's breakfast bar, my mom jotted my birthday down on an old piece of mail and quickly started adding numbers together. As she took my birthday and added the numbers together, she declared I was a number eight.

"What does an eight mean? How did you just calculate that?"

"Life Path Numbers are calculated by adding your birth month, your birth date, and the year you were born together until you get a single-digit number. There are numerology calculators online if you don't want to do the math."

With her numerology book in hand, she said, "As an eight, you are an ambitious and natural leader who has a strong ability to make money and make a difference in the world through your hardworking and entrepreneurial spirit. You need to be careful with money because you have a strong desire for it and are wired with a scarcity mindset. You seek to have power and control, and you are here to find balance."

I was so intrigued that a silly number could reveal so much about me and that the description of my Life Path Number was so accurate.

*How can a stupid number tell me so much about myself?*

Money instilled a drive in me and provided me with the control and security I craved. As a kid, when I was asked whether I'd like to play sports or get a job, I chose to get a job because I wanted to make money. I was a saver and had a difficult time spending and donating money. At one point, I was so controlling with money that I even forced my husband to carry around a notepad and document every single thing he bought, noting the exact price. My Life Path Number provided me with intel that allowed me to be more conscious of the relationship I had with money and began to heal some of my control and security issues.

And then there was the Personalysis assessment at another corporate job. Personalysis is a tool that provides you with insights into how you think, feel, and deal with the world around you. It helps clarify how you leverage your strengths while managing your blind spots. The assessment allowed me to see myself in an objective manner and provided clarity around how stress affects my life.

When I took the Personalysis assessment, I was in the trenches of trying to find answers to what I was passionate about and what my purpose was. Once again, I lost myself reviewing the results. This time, the report didn't get shoved in a drawer. Instead, I explored the report in depth. I instinctively gathered any test that I had ever taken and pieced together my results. Each personality test deepened my self-awareness and increased the power within me. I could clearly see my strengths, blind spots, desires, and fears.

Looking back at my journey, personality tests, astrology, and numerology were significant breadcrumbs. Yet I completely missed most of them because I was moving a thousand miles per hour. As I began to train my mind and body to pay attention, I began to see all of the breadcrumbs. I even started to follow them, even though some of them were big and scared the shit out of me—like speaking in front of a large group and leading a group through a self-discovery exercise.

I had developed passion and energy for self-discovery and decided to learn more about the various tools available that could aid me in my self-discovery process. I discovered tools like How to Fascinate, Enneagram, DiSC, Myers-Briggs, along with astrology-based assessments like Human Design and Gene Keys.

My favorite is Human Design, which is a detailed blueprint of your life that helps reveal your conscious and unconscious makeup. It is like an inner guidance system that provides techniques for enhancing your life. Enneagram is a close second, as it provides a holistic picture of how you think, feel, and behave based on your core fears and desires.

Personality tests served not only as a tool that enriched my self-discovery process by highlighting my blind spots and strengths, but they were also my breadcrumbs. They energized my soul and helped facilitate my passions and purpose to discover me! These breadcrumbs showed that I am passionate about self-discovery, not only for myself but for others too.

## REFLECTIVE QUESTIONS
- List ten things that bring you joy, excite you, or fascinate you.
- When you lose track of time, what are you doing?
- Name three things that break your heart.

## GROWTH EXERCISE
- Take a personality test and carefully review the results. Refer to the Resources section for a list of options.

# CHAPTER 19

# I SURRENDER

———

*"The ultimate act of power is surrender."*

KRISHNA DAS

It had been over three years since the palm reading where I had been asked the million-dollar question that always seemed to be at the forefront of my mind.

*What am I passionate about?*

I spent countless hours thinking about what it could be, had several conversations with others, and even hired a life coach and trainers to help me figure it out. My self-discovery journey significantly improved my life and helped me in so many ways. I became more conscious of my unconscious behaviors and thoughts. It allowed me to tailor my actions more closely to my actual desires and allowed me to truly heal. Despite all of the positive shifts I made, deep down, I was still irritated that I couldn't figure out what I was passionate about.

Merriam-Webster Dictionary defines passion as "an intense desire or enthusiasm for something."

Sure, I absolutely love eating food and enjoy cooking for family and friends, but I certainly wasn't passionate, nor did I have a desire to be a chef. I really enjoy planning and hosting parties, but becoming an event planner was not my calling. I found myself going down this rabbit hole time and time again, trying to find my true passion and purpose only to be left still looking for more.

Despite occasionally diving down the passion rabbit hole, I was living my life freely because I learned how to be my own friend. I was able to get out of my own way. Vibrationally, I felt like I was flying high.

On an ordinary Wednesday, my kids and I were driving to day care and jamming out to music in the car when the thought crossed through my mind.

*What are you passionate about?*

As I pulled into the day care parking lot, another thought hit me out of nowhere.

*You don't need a "thing" to be passionate about! Your passion is you and how you show up for yourself and others with so much light and love!*

It felt as if fireworks were going off in broad daylight— and not a regular show, but the grand finale. Knowing my passion felt so liberating! As I got out of the car, the sun was shining so brightly on the body of water across the street that it glistened with beauty. The serene, bright visual matched what I was feeling inside. I squeezed my kids, showered them with kisses, and walked out of the day care smiling ear to ear. I realized that I am my own special ingredient—different from anyone else—and that I get to go sprinkle myself on everyone I meet.

**My passion is being me!**

This extra spark of lightness allowed me to show up in a bigger and brighter way as my daily intention became to spread more light and love to myself and others. When I got back in my car, I immediately called one of my coaches to share the news that my passion had just discovered me. I surrendered to having an external thing.

Before, having things in order and under control reduced my anxiety. This temporarily made me feel better by giving me a false sense of reality that things were stable and okay. In some instances, seeking control enabled me not to feel my emotions and feelings. When things felt under control, there was no need for introspection because everything felt fine. When things felt out of control, I was so busy taking action to prevent certain things from happening that there was no time to feel. I found myself constantly cleaning the house, starting new projects, working extra hours, and planning trips or weekend events. The constant act of doing and overanalyzing everything kept me so busy that any feelings were shoved down into a tight box. Ignoring them gave me a false sense of control to focus on what was in front of me and what I could do to make the feelings go away.

Little by little, I noticed that I practiced surrendering to various things. It didn't happen overnight, and I found that the key to my success was taking one step at a time.

The first major thing that I surrendered to was trying to control my parents' actions as we watched my brother fall prey to the drug epidemic. I'd call my parents for information because it made me feel better to be in the know. Yet I'd find myself feeling worse after I spoke to them since they wouldn't listen to what I suggested. I judged them for their actions, thinking my way was the right way. It was a sick cycle, so I went to Nar-Anon, which is a twelve-step program for friends and family members who are affected by someone else's addiction. The meetings helped me realize that I was just adding more pain to the situation since everything was completely out of my control. The only control I had was over myself. So I began to let go. I sent out loving vibrations that my brother could heal. I started to limit conversations with my parents about my brother and what they were doing to help him.

Each time I surrendered, I could feel the resistance in my mind and body evaporate. It was as if I was able to flow with life with more ease and peace. When I'd find myself surrendering, I would ask myself, "What is it that the Universe is trying to teach me? What am I supposed to learn from the situation?" Sometimes when I wasn't sure, I'd find myself reciting the serenity prayer:

> God grant me the serenity
> to accept the things I cannot change,
> courage to change the things I can,
> and wisdom to know the difference.

The serenity prayer always helps ground me and assists me today when my need for control resurfaces.

I also surrendered to the fact that I didn't need to know everything to add value and be good at what I did and that I could quit my job at any time. I surrendered the need for others' validation or approval because I was so clear on who I was and what I wanted. I surrendered to the fact that taking risks wasn't always dangerous. I surrendered that while I can help care for my dad, I am not responsible for his health and happiness. I surrendered that having a messy house is just as okay as having a clean one. In fact, leaving the house messy for a few days became one of my best tests to exercise my control muscle. I surrendered that I don't have control over anyone else's journey in this life other than my own. American author Tom Bodett said, "In school, you're taught a lesson and then given a test. In life, you're given a test that teaches you a lesson." The quote resonates with my soul because I've learned that planet Earth is our school. Living each and every day to the fullest and with passion is the true test. In order to do that, we must surrender so that we can learn our life lessons as we move into pure awareness.

The biggest lesson I learned was to surrender. Yet I also had to learn the tools to work through my false beliefs, imposter syndrome, fears around money, and learning how to take risks and exercise my mind to allow for rest versus adhering to what I thought I *should* be doing.

The act of surrendering allows me to tap into my heart space—a space that I had not accessed because my mind was too busy running the show. Each time I found myself surrendering, I could feel my inner power strengthening. It was as if the invisible weights I was carrying around were being removed one at a time. I know that when I can exercise my mind and body to be still enough to listen, I am able to guide myself in the direction I am meant to go. The act of surrendering is an extreme form of acknowledgment. Surrendering is the epitome of unconditional love. Looking back, I didn't find it ironic that the moment I surrendered to searching for an external passion outside of myself was when the magic really started to happen.

## REFLECTIVE QUESTIONS

- Name two areas in your life where you feel the most resistance or continue to repeat a negative pattern that doesn't serve you. Is it time to surrender?
- How can you spread light and love to yourself? What about to others?
- Where can you afford yourself grace?

## GROWTH EXERCISES:

- Pick one thing that is no longer serving you. Visualize yourself surrendering it. How would you feel? Be as descriptive as possible as you visualize yourself doing this.
- Say the serenity prayer out loud.

---

---

---

---

---

---

---

---

---

---

---

---

---

---

---

---

---

# CHAPTER 20

# LET THE MAGIC HAPPEN

---

*"The wound is where the light enters."*

RUMI

I taught the Universe how I wanted to be treated. Each morning, I cultivate a strong routine and stay present, listening to what my mind, body, and spirit need. My divine imprints no longer run me because I am aware of them. My five-minute morning affirmation has developed into two hours of time to just *be*. Mornings vary depending on what I need. I find myself reading, moving my body, doing yoga or a work out, journaling, sitting outside while drinking coffee, reciting affirmations, or meditating. I even allow myself to sleep in if that is what my body needs. My morning routine is rejuvenating, and it sets my day up for success. Even on days when I only have five minutes, rarely do I miss a morning.

I feel light. I have clarity and find humor each day. I am full of energy for the exact same life I was previously living when I used to feel drained and unfulfilled. I find myself pausing to feel the breeze of the fresh air, savoring the hint of cinnamon in my coffee, hearing the birds chirp, and seeing my kids' ways of being as pure magic. I am living with complete integrity and honoring what I actually desire, without the need to control anything. I know I am divinely supported and enough. Over time, my morning practice and affirmations rewired the neuron pathways in my brain, allowing me to stay present, which keep my anxiety and false beliefs at bay.

I found myself writing in an "I AM" journal to manifest burning desires. Written words, such as "I am a passionate, powerful, present, and peaceful leader who is whole and complete and an instrument of divine light and love" would make their way onto the page each morning. I would then speak those words out loud to hear my strong voice. I would go on to create three intentional daily actions with the goal of spreading and attracting more light and love in my life. I found that my actions would mirror my "I AM" statement.

It was as if the Universe was conspiring to work with me. The job that allowed me to hit rock bottom, the same job that I was going to quit, became a stepping-stone to a job that more closely aligns with my strengths, values, and desires. Each day, I exercise my mind to follow my heart, keeping a sharp eye out for breadcrumbs. I've fostered an inner knowing and belief system that whatever comes my way, I am more than capable of handling. I am so clear on who I am and what I desire that letting others down rarely affects me. I am living each day, trusting the process, and flowing with life. I've healed parts of myself that I didn't even realize required healing, allowing me to become free, which has increased my energy and allowed me to attract what I want into my life.

Since I had created space in my life by saying "no" to the things that did not feel like breadcrumbs, in 2019 I found myself spending my Christmas break learning how to facilitate an exercise that I would present to my colleagues shortly after the new year. Time and time again, I found myself losing track of time while practicing how to facilitate the exercise, reading how to do it, and telling everyone I knew about it.

*Why am I excited to speak in public? I hate that shit!*

Facilitation day approached quickly. I boarded a plane headed for Texas feeling giddy, excited, and confident as I read the magazine that sat in the seat pocket in front of me. I looked at my phone and the time read 9:00 a.m. I had two hours to get to the corporate headquarters. I grabbed my carry-on and quickly secured an Uber. As we drove down the interstate, I looked out the window in pure delight. All of a sudden, chills began to run up and down my body like wildfire, as I felt the clearest message being presented to me.

*Lauren, your passion and purpose is helping others learn more about themselves through the self-discovery process, guiding them to move past their blocks and empowering them to show up as their true authentic selves, so their passions and purpose can discover them!*

The biggest smile washed over my face. I unzipped my carry-on suitcase that sat on the seat to my left and reached for my "I AM" journal to write down the clear message that came through to me. In big bold words, I wrote down, "MY PASSION JUST DISCOVERED ME!"

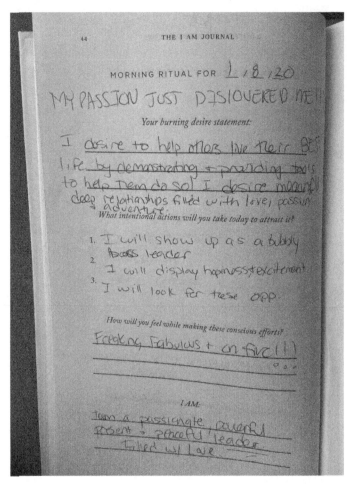

MORNING RITUAL FOR 1 / 8 / 20

MY PASSION JUST DISCOVERED ME!!

*Your burning desire statement:*

I desire to help others live their best
life by demonstrating + providing tools
to help them do so! I desire meaningful
deep relationships filled with love, passion
adventure.

*What intentional actions will you take today to attract it?*

1. I will show up as a bubbly
2. boss leader
   I will display happiness, excitement
3. I will look for these opp.

*How will you feel while making these conscious efforts?*

Freaking Fabulous + on fire!!

*I AM.*

I am a passionate, powerful
present + peaceful leader
filled w/ love

My journal entry the day my passion and purpose discovered me

I felt like I had been lit on fire! It wasn't long before I was standing alone, front and center, in the middle of the conference room, providing instructions to my peers, leaders, and even a few unicorns. I was no longer taking instructions; I was giving them. The exercise was a hit, and a few people came up to me afterward expressing gratitude for what it allowed them to see. My breadcrumbs had officially turned into a full-blown meal! I wasn't sure where to go with my new insight, but I felt called to take more aligned action, even though many of my ideas scared the shit out of me.

Not more than two weeks went by before I was inspired to create an Instagram handle, coining myself as the "Mind Muscle Motivator." I realized that my mind was like a muscle. If I wanted it to be healthy and strong, it required daily exercise so that it would serve me. Instagram provided me with an immediate opportunity to take action and share my light and love, along with the wisdom and tools I had picked up along my inward quest.

Each morning, I found myself called to write inspirational posts. It was as if something was taking over my fingers; the words flowed effortlessly.

*How can this be? Me, a writer? Why isn't writing hard for me anymore? Why do I like it?*

I realized that through my inward quest, I had lifted a chest full of heavy weight off me. I was free! Writing is therapeutic and serves as a mechanism to share my light and love with others. With so much gratitude for living my life with such intention and purpose, I decided to disrupt my new normal even further. For my thirty-fifth birthday, instead of drinking with friends over dinner, I signed myself up for another weekend training called "Grace." It was three sacred days where I practiced leading with my body instead of my mind while tapping into my intuitive wisdom and power within.

We were instructed to bring various items, one being a journal. I went to my nightstand full of blank journals and grabbed the one that said, "Be STRONG and COURAGEOUS

—Deuteronomy 31:6." As I removed it from my nightstand, a folded piece of paper fell onto the ground. I picked it up and unfolded it. It was the same piece of paper the Passionate Palmist handed me years earlier that had sent me down this inward quest.

As I began to read what the piece of paper said, tears started falling down my cheeks. It read, "Your life's purpose is to be of service. A passionate leader/role model who takes action for her people through creative communication to make a difference." The same words that I couldn't understand four years prior now made complete sense.

It was a humbling and magical moment, considering the Mind Muscle Motivator was created for just that. I used to hate it when I'd hear people say that everything happens for a reason or that you are exactly where you are supposed to be, but in that exact moment, I understood. My self-discovery process helped me realize that we all have hidden gems buried within us. Some we aren't even aware of or haven't fully expressed since they are covered by limiting beliefs, fears, and past traumas that hijack our power. When I became conscious and took action to move past the things that were holding me back, I was able to align my mind, body, and spirit. It allowed me to live purely from my heart space. Living from my heart space allows my creativity and hidden gems to shine.

I've found that it takes the consistent exercise of the mind to truly witness yourself with raw honesty and allow for healing to take place. The heart knows what the mind cannot understand, but in order to get there, the mind must be mastered. Our passions and purpose discover us through the self-discovery process.

The thought of guiding others to master their mind so their passions and purpose can reveal themselves continues to bring chills to my body. It fills my heart up with gratitude and purpose, knowing that life is a journey, not a destination, and that I am now embarking on an adventure of a lifetime.

NOW is the time to get off your hamster wheel and go within!

Create your sacred time and continue to build off it as you exercise your mind to serve you.

Allow for grace, knowing that nothing happens overnight.

Give yourself the love that you so freely give to everyone else around you.

The world needs *your* hidden gems, passions, and purpose to shine!

## REFLECTIVE QUESTIONS

- List one action step you will take to get off your hamster wheel.
- What is the biggest takeaway you had from reading this book so that you can allow magic to happen in your life?

## GROWTH EXERCISE

- Go to mindmusclemotivator.com for additional reflective questions that are paired with each chapter.

# RESOURCES

**BOOKS THAT INSPIRE ME:**

- Armstrong, Alison. *Keys to the Kingdom.*
- Bernstein, Gabrielle. *The Universe Has Your Back.*
- Brooks, Rachel. *Chasing Perfection.*
- Brown, Brené. *Dare to Lead.*
- Brown, Brené. *Rising Strong.*
- Bunnell, Lynda and Ra Urh Hu. *The Definitive Book of Human Design.*
- Byrne, Rhonda. *The Secret.*
- Cameron, Julia. *The Artist's Way.*
- Chopra, Deepak. *The Seven Spiritual Laws of Success.*
- Curry, Karen. *Understanding Human Design.*
- Dispenza, Joe. *Breaking the Habit of Being Yourself.*
- Doyle, Glennon. *Untamed.*
- Dyer, Wayne. *Being in Balance.*
- Elrod, Hal. *The Miracle Morning.*
- Eurich, Tasha. *Insight.*
- Gilbert, Elizabeth. *Big Magic.*
- Gilbert, Elizabeth. *Eat, Pray, Love.*
- Hardy, Darren. *The Compound Effect.*

- Hay, Louise. *The Power Is Within You.*
- Hay, Louise. *You Can Heal Your Life.*
- Hicks, Esther and Jerry Hicks. *The Law of Attraction.*
- Lama, Dalai and Desmond Tutu. *The Book of Joy.*
- Laube, Marga. *Agents of Evolution.*
- LePera, Nicole. *How to Do the Work.*
- Lee, Chris. *Transform Your Life: 10 Principles of Abundance & Prosperity*
- Mason, Mark. *The Subtle Art of Not Giving a F*ck.*
- McConaughey, Matthew. *Greenlights.*
- Nichols, Lisa. *Abundance Now.*
- Nichols, Lisa. *No Matter What!*
- Obama, Michelle. *Becoming.*
- Rose, Sahara. *Discover Your Dharma.*
- Rudd, Richard. *The Gene Keys.*
- Ruiz, Miguel. *The Four Agreements.*
- Sher, Barbara. *I Could Do Anything If Only I knew What It Was.*
- Shetty, Jay. *Think Like a Monk.*
- Simpson, Jessica. *Open Book.*
- Sincero, Jen. *You are a Badass Every Day.*
- Singer, Michael. *The Surrender Experiment.*
- Tolle, Eckert. *The Power of Now.*
- Winfrey, Oprah and Bruce Perry. *What Happened to You?*
- Young, Valerie. *Secret Thoughts of Successful Women*
- Walsh, Regan. *Heart Boss.*

**PERSONALITY TESTS:**
- Clifton StrengthsFinder—www.gallup.com/cliftonstrengths
- DiSC—www.123test.com
- Enneagram—www.truity.com

- How to Fascinate—www.howtofascinate.com
- Jung Typology Test—www.humanmetrics.com
- Personalysis—www.personalysis.wiredtothrive.com

**ASTROLOGY:**
- Gene Keys—www.genekeys.com
- Human Design—www.jovianarchive.com
- Life Path Numbers—www.numerology.center/life

# ACKNOWEDGMENTS

---

A huge thank you to everyone who made this book possible!

To my amazing beta readers, thank you!

- Amy Bull, for your thoughtful feedback and enthusiasm.
- Andrea Hanners, for being my right-hand woman and constant support system.
- Blair Thomas, for always being my rose.
- Erin Greely, for doing my homework and your creative ideas.
- Jackie Hoffbuhr, for your selfless offer and lending your expertise.
- Jenna Brader, for your special gifts and sacred time.
- John Hopkins, for your humor and southern sass.
- Lindsey Morton, for your attention to detail and creating space for this special project.
- Mariko Frederick, for your wisdom and living out your soul's priority.
- Meera Patel, for being an amazing friend and boss.

- My busy colleagues, Lauren Coleman and Regina Farmer, for making the time to read my entire manuscript. God bless you both.
- My honest and loving sister, Kate Vazquez, for your unwavering support, honest feedback, and talking through difficult chapters.
- My husband, Brian, for allowing me to share part of our story and for listening to me read every chapter.
- Nicole Farrell, for your generosity and kindness. There are no accidents in life.
- Stacie Stormer, for your willingness and patience.
- Stephanie Worley, for answering my fifty million questions.
- Simone McKenna, for being the first beta reader to jump in.
- Tiffany Harlan, for your light and encouragement.

To everyone at the Creator Institute, especially Eric Koester for your vision and Haley Newlin for your bubbly support.

Thank you to everyone at New Degree Press for allowing me to share my light and love through this book. This book would not have been possible without the special assistance from the following:
- Christine Rich, for being a kick-ass accountability partner.
- John Saunders, for waiting on the other end while I got my shit together.
- Katherine Mazoyer, for your positivity and for going above and beyond.
- Katie Sigler, for your thoughtful feedback and open mind.
- Lisa Patterson, for your guidance and recommendations.
- Tasslyn Magnusson, for your time and consideration.

A special thanks to the following:

- Adrienne Hasty, for your vibrancy and making the introduction.
- Ann Bogenrief, for your honesty and love.
- April McClanahan, for being a light when I needed it most.
- Chris Hawker, Chris Lee, Krista Petty, Kathy McKenzie, and Eric Clark, for your dedication to people and their transformation.
- Debbie Krasnodembski, for being our COVID-19 teacher and keeping me sane enough to write this book.
- Debe Turnbull, for asking me the question that changed the trajectory of my life.
- Elisa Ballantyne, for embodying confidence at such a young age and protecting your people.
- Erin Washington, for being an inspiration and showing me I could write a book too.
- Faith Knight Myers, Karen Johnson, and Sandra Gardinier, for being unicorns and seeing the light in me.
- Grandaddy, for all of the traditions.
- Grandmother, for teaching me your special ways.
- Joe and Martha Wolfe, Taylor Katzenstein, and Julie Keller, for always being breaths of fresh air.
- Lizzie Vance, for setting me up for writing success.
- Madeline Lee, for the money shot.
- Marga Laube, for following your passion and your time.
- Mark Osoteo, for planting a seed.
- My immediate and extended family, for all of your love.
- Next Level community, especially Tonia Pettus, Elaine Bell, Helaina Pearce, Salt & Pepper, Epic Diamonds, and

the White Angels, for your openness and willingness to go on a wild ride together.

- Schlaine Hutchinson, for being my angel.
- The University of Dayton and Ohio Northern University Petit College of Law, for thinking outside of the box and taking a chance on me.
- Tony Morelli, for your ultimate sacrifice.
- Uncle Kenny Bob, for your one-liner imprint.
- Valerie Young, EdD, for your research and time.
- 108 Evantson, for your energy and compassion.

And finally, thank you to my VIP Reclaim Your Power Supporters: Abbie France, Aimee Corney, Aishwarya Singh, Alexis Michalovich, Amanda Brasser, Amanda Clark, Amanda Pavolino, Amber Coleman, Amber Mott, Amy Bull, Amy Hill, Amy Zacharias, Andrea Hanners, Andrew Thomas, Angela Han, Angela Woessner, Ann Bogenrief, Annette McMurry, Anthony Coffman, April McClanahan, Ashley Morelock, Ashley Oliker, Ashley Stankovik, Ashley Warner, Barb Kennedy, Ben Stormer, Beverly Oddi, Blair Thomas, Brandy Fournet, Brandy Jemczura, Breanne Boeke, Brenda Hanyak, Brian Krasnodembski, Brittany Krasnodembski, Camille Cunningham, Casey Cargill, Chandra Carson, Christi Cooper, Christina Penzinski, Christine Rich, Cortney Fargo, Courtney Gerber, Courtney Bodkin, Courtney Kidd, Crissa Clark, Cynthia Cartwright, Dana Reisinger, David Kimball, Debbie Krasnodembski, Denise Jones, Desmond Dunham, Diane Sacks, Donna Richardson, Drew Weizer, Ed Daniels, Elisa Ballantyne, Elizabeth Gay, Emily Carben, Emily Clegg, Eric Clark, Eric Koester, Erica Sylvis, Erin Keel, Eun Holly, Eva Borsai, Faith Knight Myers, Gary Cacciatore, Gina Piacentino, Heather Curry, Hollie Foust,

Iliana Peters, Irene Slabaugh, Isaiah Shalwitz, Jackie Hoffbuhr, Jackie Perucki, Jackie Yoder, Jamie Johnson, Janet Foo, Jennifer Bazemore, Jennifer Ciszewski, Jennifer Doubrava, Jennifer Meyer, Jessica Frank, Jessica Quesada, Jill Hoffman, Jillian Monahan, Joe Wolfe, John Fuhrer, John Hanyak, John Hopkins, John White, Julie Hoy, Julie Keller, Kanika Sloan, Karen Hammer, Karen Smith, Kate Vazquez, Kathleen Morris, Kathy Houck, Kathy Mckenzie, Katie Finnegan, Katie Kenney, Katie Minister, Kelly Rodenfels, Kelsey Ostrander, Kelsi Hersha, Kenneth Gay, Kieshia Devezin, Kim Diehl-Boyd, Kimberly Chapman, Kris Stolz, Kristi Daiker, Krysten Criss, Laura Smith, Lilla Toth, Linda Hanyak, Lindsay Miller, Lindsey Morton, Lisa Acevedo-Hutcheson, Liz Otley, Lloyd Leppert, Lori Havlovitz, Lyndale Reisinger, Martha Wolfe, Madeline Lee, Maggie Greene, Marcela Kratochvilova, Marcia Rausch, Marcie Mauro, Maria Groh, Marian Lerner, Mariko Frederick, Marisa Billips, Mark Mosley, Mark Osoteo, Martha Russell, Mary Agbovi, Mary Beth Schrudder, Mary Jane Bayer, Meera Patel, Meghan McCurdy, Michael Krasnodembski, Michelle Leyland, Michelle Muthiani, Michelle Vazquez, Miranda Gill, Missi Hart-Kothari, Nancy Dorner, Nicole Farrell, Nicole Galiardi, Nicole Johnson, Nicole Morris, Nilu Ekanayake, Norma Vazquez, Patricia Kervin, Patty Glandorf, Preetha Sridhar, Rachell Kitchen, Rick Bayer, Robert Giacalone, Roshal Marshall, Rose Eugene, Russell Nelson, Rusten May, Sara Gaul, Sarah Flanigan, Schlaine Hutchins, Scott Gaines, Scott Krasnodembski, Shannon Clegg, Shatora Gilchrist, Stacie Stormer, Stephanie Marburger, Stephanie Martinez, Stephanie Patterson, Stephanie Pugh, Stephanie Worley, Stu Kim, Susan Sloan, Taylor Katzenstein, Thomas Jacko, Tiffany Harlan, Tiffany Mosher, Toni Gotter, Tony Reese, Traci Mitchell, Ty Sonagere, Ursula Johnson, Vanessa

Hooper, Victoria Hutta, Victoria Strelnikova, and Whitney Osborne.

# APPENDIX

---

**INTRODUCTION**

Clifton, Jim. "The World's Broken Workplace." *The Chairman's Blog* (blog). June 13, 2017. https://news.gallup.com/opinion/chairman/212045/world-broken-workplace.aspx?g_source=position1&g_medium=related&g_campaign=tiles.

Craig, Lydia. "Are You Suffering From Imposter Syndrome?" *American Psychological Association: Psychological Science Agenda,* September 2018. https://www.apa.org/science/about/psa/2018/09/imposter-syndrome.

**CHAPTER 3**

Young, Valerie. *The Secret Thoughts of Successful Women: Why Capable People Suffer from the Imposter Syndrome and How to Thrive in Spite of it.* New York: Crown Business, 2011.

## CHAPTER 7

*AttractPassion.* "Pineal Gland Awakening with Dr. Joe Dispenza | How to Upgrade Your Brain." 2020. Video, 17:06. https://m. youtube.com/watch?v=goQOnpyzo_k.

## CHAPTER 10

Eurich, Tasha. *Insight: The Surprising Truth About How Others See Us, How We See Ourselves, and Why the Answers Matter More Than We Think.* New York: Crown Business, 2018.

Eurich, Tasha. "What Self-Awareness Really Is (and How to Cultivate It)." *Harvard Business Review.* January 4, 2018. https:// hbr.org/2018/01/what-self-awareness-really-is-and-how-to-cultivate-it.

## CHAPTER 12

Perrotta, Mike. "Controlling Your Mind by Controlling Your Breath." *Start it Up* (blog). June 10, 2020. https://medium.com/ swlh/neuroscience-of-breath-63c32604be22.

"Relaxation Techniques: Breath Control Helps Quell Errant Stress Response." *Harvard Health Blog* (blog). July 6, 2020. https:// www.health.harvard.edu/mind-and-mood/relaxation-techniques-breath-control-helps-quell-errant-stress-response.

## CHAPTER 14

MacDonald, Catherine. "A Chuckle a Day Keeps the Doctor Away: Therapeutic Humor & Laughter." *Journal of Psychosocial Nurs-*

*ing and Mental Health Services* 42, 3 (2004): 18-25. https://doi.org/10.3928/02793695-20040315-05.

## CHAPTER 16

Laube, Marga. *Agents of Evolution: An Astrological Guide for Transformative Times.* New York: New Degree Press, 2021.

## CHAPTER 19

*Merriam-Webster Dictionary.* s.v. "passion (*n.*)." Accessed May 31, 2021. https://www.merriam-webster.com/dictionary/passion.